Nehemiah Adams

Memorial Volume by the Essex Street Church and Society, Boston to Commemorate the Twenty-Fifth Anniversary of the Installation of their Pastor, Nehemiah Adams, D.D.

Nehemiah Adams

Memorial Volume by the Essex Street Church and Society, Boston to Commemorate the Twenty-Fifth Anniversary of the Installation of their Pastor, Nehemiah Adams, D.D.

ISBN/EAN: 9783337715656

Printed in Europe, USA, Canada, Australia, Japan

Cover: Foto ©Lupo / pixelio.de

More available books at **www.hansebooks.com**

Memorial Volume

BY THE

ESSEX STREET CHURCH AND SOCIETY

BOSTON

TO COMMEMORATE THE

TWENTY-FIFTH ANNIVERSARY

OF THE

INSTALLATION OF THEIR PASTOR

NEHEMIAH ADAMS, D.D.

BOSTON
PRINTED FOR THE USE OF THE MEMBERS
1860

RIVERSIDE, CAMBRIDGE:
PRINTED BY H. O. HOUGHTON AND COMPANY.

Preliminaries.

CELEBRATION

OF THE

TWENTY-FIFTH ANNIVERSARY

OF THE

PASTOR'S SETTLEMENT.

———◆———

PRELIMINARIES.

SEVERAL members of the Union (Essex Street) Church and Society were informally invited, December, 1858, by one of their number, to meet at the house of Deacon Charles Scudder, to confer with regard to a celebration of the Twenty-Fifth Anniversary of the Pastor's Settlement.

At this meeting, various Committees were appointed to make suitable arrangements for a celebration.

On the fifteenth of February, a printed notice was sent to all the present and past members of the Church and Society, so far as they could be ascertained, by the Committee on Invitations, informing them of the proposed services, and inviting those at a distance to accept the hospitalities of our families, if they should attend. Invitations were also sent by the Committee, and through the Pastor, to numerous clergymen and laymen, and to the classmates of Doctor ADAMS in Harvard College and the Andover Theological Seminary.

PREPARATORY RELIGIOUS EXERCISES.

The Church, by appointment, observed Friday, March twenty-fifth, as a day of special prayer in view of the past, and also with reference to the approaching anniversary services, — meeting in the Lecture Room in the afternoon, and a lecture preparatory to the Lord's Supper being preached by the Pastor in the evening. The administration of the Lord's Supper took place one Sabbath earlier than usual, to afford opportunity of communion at the table of Christ with former members of the Church who might be in attendance.

Saturday, the twenty-sixth of March, being the Anniversary of Installation, the Pastor, on Sabbath morning, the twenty-seventh, preached a Sermon commemorative of his settlement, from Genesis xxxi. 13 (a part of the verse): "I am the God of Bethel, where thou anointedst the pillar, and where thou vowedst a vow unto me." In the afternoon, practical remarks were made by the Pastor from the same words, and the Lord's Supper was administered. Three individuals made a public profession of their faith in Christ.

In the evening of the Sabbath a meeting for prayer and conference was held, at which were present several early members of the Church. Reminiscences of its history, and accounts of the character and labors of some of its founders and their associates, were related.

Exercises at the Anniversary.

EXERCISES AT THE ANNIVERSARY.

Monday evening, March twenty-eighth, was the time appointed for the public celebration. John Tappan, Esquire, presided.

The following Selections from the Scriptures were chanted by the Choir: —

"I have set watchmen upon thy walls, O Jerusalem, which shall never hold their peace, day nor night. Ye that make mention of the Lord, keep not silence."

"The chariots of God are twenty thousand, even thousands of angels; the Lord is among them as in Sinai, in the holy place. Thou hast ascended on high, thou hast led captivity captive, thou hast received gifts for men; yea, for the rebellious also, that the Lord God might dwell among them."

"And he gave some, apostles, and some, prophets, and some, evangelists, and some, pastors and teachers, for the perfecting of the saints, for the work of the ministry, for the edifying of the body of Christ."

"Be thou faithful unto death, and I will give thee a crown of life."

"How beautiful upon the mountains are the feet of him that bringeth good tidings, that publisheth peace; that bringeth good tidings of good, that publisheth salvation; that saith unto Zion, Thy God reigneth."

"His foundation is in the holy mountains.

"The Lord loveth the gates of Zion more than all the dwellings of Jacob.

"Glorious things are spoken of thee, O city of God.

"I will make mention of Rahab and Babylon to them that know me; behold Philistia, and Tyre, with Ethiopia; this man was born there.

"And of Zion it shall be said, This and that man was born in her; and the highest himself shall establish her.

"The Lord shall count, when he writeth up the people, that this man was born there.

"As well the singers, as the players on instruments, shall be there; all my springs are in thee."

The Reverend SAMUEL M. WORCESTER, Pastor of the Tabernacle Church in Salem, where our Pastor was baptized by the elder Doctor Worcester, led in prayer.

ODE.

ANNIVERSARY OF TWENTY-FIVE YEARS AGO.

CHANT ADAPTED BY EDWARD HAMILTON. ("THE LORD IS MY SHEPHERD.")

THE following ODE, written by Mrs. REBECCA W. DAVIES, of New York, a former Member of this Church, (daughter of John Tappan, Esquire,) was chanted by the Choir: —

SOFTLY, softly, toll the bell,
That calls us to the House of Prayer!
What do its chiming accents tell,
Ringing on the vernal air?
" Passing away! Passing away!"
To our hearts they seem to say.
Days and weeks, with flying tread,
Months and years have quickly sped
Since we stood, in joyful bands,
At our youthful Pastor's side,
Pledging him our hearts and hands,
Choosing him — a heavenward guide.

Childhood's rosy bloom has faded;
Sunny brows with grief been shaded;
Raven locks are tinged with snow;
All is changing fast, below.

   Sadly, sadly, toll the bell!
Memory wakes her phantom host,
Calls from out her dreamy cell
Visions of the loved and lost.
Matron fair, and maiden sweet,
Brother, son, we seem to meet;
Loved companions, to our side,
Swift, with noiseless footsteps, glide.
Alas! we know the green grass waves
Calmly o'er their silent graves.
The tear will fall, the heart will swell,
As we hear that mournful bell.
While it sadly seems to say,—
" All we love shall pass away!"

Sweetly, sweetly, toll the bell!
Call it not a funeral knell.
Hark! what heavenly cadence floats,
Mingling with our earthly notes.
Father, mother, sister, friend,
From their radiant mansions bend,
Whispering, in each drooping ear,—
" Weep not that we are not here.
By our Saviour's presence blest,
On the heavenly hills we rest;

With celestial manna fed,
Near the throne of light above,
By the crystal waters led,
Loved with more than mortal love;
Still we fondly hover round
What to us is hallowed ground;
Watching, in the House of Prayer,
All your songs of praise we share."

Saviour! when our work is o'er,
May we hope to reach that shore?
Hope, in peace, at thy right hand,
Pastor, people, all to stand?
Never more to say farewell,
Nor with sadness hear that bell;
Though it still shall seem to say,
"All of earth shall pass away."

Addresses.

ADDRESSES.

REMARKS BY THE CHAIRMAN.

THE Chairman, JOHN TAPPAN, Esquire, spoke as follows: —

RESPECTED BRETHREN AND FRIENDS:

It is my pleasant duty, in behalf of the Union Church and Society, to welcome you to this Celebration of the Twenty-fifth Anniversary of our Pastor's Settlement. We thank you for joining us in ascriptions of praise to Almighty God, for the gift of a Shepherd who has faithfully preached the faith once delivered to the Saints, — the power of God and the wisdom of God unto salvation, to all who believe and obey. How he has gone in and out before us, these loving hearts will testify; and, in their behalf, it is my happiness to assure you that the tie which binds Pastor and People is a threefold cord, which death alone can break. We ask you to join us in the prayer, that it will please the great Head of the Church to grant that he may long be upheld in standing up for Jesus in this consecrated Temple, and in all the surrounding Churches.

I have now the pleasure of introducing to you our beloved and respected associate, whose voice is music to all our ears, — the Honorable RUFUS CHOATE.

ADDRESS

BY HONORABLE RUFUS CHOATE.

I FEEL myself obliged to confess, and I am sure you will allow me to confess, that in feeling willing to take some very humble part in the services of this evening, I have been influenced partly, I have no doubt, by a consideration which is personal; and that is, that it happens to be about five and twenty years since I became a resident in Boston and connected myself with the Society which now observes this anniversary, very shortly after the inauguration of this clergyman; which event has been attended with so much at once of instruction and pleasure, to all of us who have had an opportunity to hear his ministrations since. Invited, therefore, in some sort, to take part in my own ecclesiastical silver wedding, I could hardly decline to do so even if I had loved him less, or had been less attached to the Society itself than I certainly avow myself to be. That principle of our nature which attaches much importance to what interests ourselves, whether others think much of it or not, and which enables us to hold on forever upon what has been once our own — this alone, if there were nothing other and better, I hope would have made me willing and made me happy to have said something, without much preparation, to-night.

And yet, even so, the predominant impression in my own mind, and in every one's mind under the circumstances, probably is, the difficulty of making it real to one's self that so vast a portion of human life has sped away, as it might seem, like a dream in the night, like a dream when a man awakes. If we were permitted to look beyond these endeared old walls to the great, busy, and crowded world without, in order to take an estimate of the lapse of time; if we could be permitted here, for example, to remember in regard to our own country, that within that comparatively brief period nine Presidents of the United States have acted their part upon that high stage, — that so many administrations of government have followed one another in that high place, — that we have endured, I know not how many, half a dozen, eight or nine, national or party conflicts — that we have in that short time enlarged our territory by an area equal to that of France and Germany and Austria together — that we have flown up from four and twenty to, I think, two and thirty, or three and thirty, States; if we could be permitted to cross the ocean, and remember that one nation, the greatest but one in the world, has in that time changed its government twice, fundamentally, passing from the apparent love of liberty and the apparent forms of a Republic to a despotism, gloomy, peculiar, established, although it hangs but upon one man's life; that in another country, the first or the second in the Old World, six English ministers have risen and fallen upon the ebb and flow of English conservative freedom; that an infusion of fresh revolutionary or democratic elements has swept away Church and State, as it were, almost altogether, and that the Old England of our fathers has become the New England of to-day; if we could be permitted to call to mind, also, with what winged progress science and art have sped upward in that time, what new stars have been added by the telescope to our sky, new processes to our invention, new fields opened to our benevolence and our philanthropy, and the general progress so brilliant and so rich, which has marked the flight of years — it might, perhaps, enable us to appreciate it better. Personal reasons, if it were proper to allude to them, would enable us to make that impression still more deep. But then looking about on these walls, so familiar to us alone, remarking these familiar and dear faces, listening as we usually do, to these Sabbath tones of prayer and music, perhaps we can better express the impression which all of it makes upon us in the simple phrase of Cowper:

> "Dear school-mate, five and twenty years ago!
> Alas! how time escapes us — even so!"

And yet this period is a large section of the life of man; and perhaps one inquiry, — a leading inquiry for a thoughtful person under the circumstances in which we meet, — is, what account can we give of ourselves? If we were interrogated as to the manner in which we have spent it, what account can we give of ourselves, for having spent it here under the ministrations to which we have been admitted? Custom, decorum, self-respect, general seriousness, and general appreciation of the personal and domestic uses of public worship, a general appreciation that this life is introductory only, and these days of ours are only periods of preparation, as well as consciousness and work, would have carried us, of course, to some congregation. But what shall we say, for ourselves, has brought us here? I have no doubt that it may have happened in many cases that accident has done it. I dare say the reasons, in some other instances, have been peculiar, or incommunicable in public. But then there are some which we may here avow and justify thus publicly, and to these I beg to call your attention for a moment.

I think, then, that every one of you would unite with me in expressing the opinion, that we have been influenced to such a course as this, in large measure, by our love and respect for our Minister. In his presence, it may not be entirely delicate that we should say about this all that we think; and I hope that we are too just, also, in the presence, and with our opinions, of the clergy of Boston, to compare or contrast one member of the learned, dignified, and most useful profession with another, publicly or privately. But, then, I may be permitted to say, for you and with you, we love and respect him. We have done so from the moment that we knew him first to this hour. We have marked the daily beauty of his life; his consistency, his steadiness, his affectionateness, his sincerity, — transparent to every eye; his abilities, his moderation, his taste, his courage. We have despised the occasional criticisms upon his daring to think upon anything, in theology or out of it, for himself. Differing, as I dare say many of us do, from him in very many things, we have yet admired, and we love to proclaim, here and now, our admiration of him who would dare philosophically to see with his own eyes, and to record under his own hand, what he personally believed to be true. Thank God, thought is free, speech is free, the press is free. To that extent, even that popularity which is worth having, — the popularity which follows, not that which is run after, — that, I believe, in some days that shall come, as my Lord Bacon so beautifully and pathetically expresses it in his will, "If not now, even that popularity shall reward and honor the search after truth, and the open and manly publication of it." Some of you have seen him, on some occasions, in some situations of life, most interesting to the feelings, and which dwell the longest in the memory and the affections. You have seen him at the bedside of the sick and dying, and at the burial of those you loved most on earth; he has baptized your children, and has handed to you, perhaps, the clasped hands of your brides. Some of you preserve yet "the little key" which clasped, in his presence, the coffin-lid of the loved young child; and thus there has been woven between you and him a tie which can never be sundered, even when the silver cord of love itself is loosened and the bowl is broken at its fountain. I unite with what our venerable Chairman has already said to you. I unite with him in saying, that while we love and admire him, very far distant be that day when his monument shall record, by the side of his grave, — " Here lies a faithful minister of Jesus Christ; " and a thousand hearts, and the tears of a thousand eyes, shall exclaim, — " Servant of God, well done!"

There is a second reason, however, it seems to me, which we may, with very great propriety, give for the selection which we have made and to which we have so long adhered; and it is, my friends, that we have attended this

Worship and attached ourselves to this Society, because we have believed that we found here a union of a true and old religion, with a possibility and the duty of a theory of culture, and of love for that in which the mental and moral nature of man may be developed and may be completely accomplished.

That we hold a specific religious creed is quite certain; obtruding it on nobody, and not for a moment, of course, dreaming of defending ourselves against anybody; in the way of our Fathers, we worship God in this Assembly. We believe that the sources and proof and authority of religion rest upon a Written Revelation, communicated by the Supreme Will to a race standing in certain specific abnormal conditions. What that Will, honestly gathered, teaches, composes the whole religious duty of man. To find out that meaning, by all the aids of which a thorough and an honest scholarship may possibly avail itself, — by the study of original tongues, by the study of the history and government and manners and customs and geography of the nations in which it was first published; by a collation, honestly and intelligently, of one version with another version; by the history of creeds; by attending especially to the faith of those Churches who thought they saw the light at first, and saw it when it was clearest and brightest, — by all this, we say, it is the first duty of the minister to learn the truth, and the second duty is to impress it by persuasive speech and holy life upon the consciences and hearts of men. These things, truly and honestly interrogated, reveal a certain state of truths, and these compose our creed and the creed of every other denomination possessing and preaching and maintaining a kindred theology. Diversities of expression there are, undoubtedly; diversities of the metaphysical theories of those who hold them; more or less saliency, more or less illustration in the mode in which they are presented. But substantially we have thought they were one. We regard the unity, and we forget the diversity, in concentration of kindred substances. I think our Church began with the name and in the principle of Union; and in that name, and according to that principle, we maintain it to-day.

And now is there anything, my friends, in all this, which is incompatible, in any degree, with the warmest and most generous and large and liberal and general culture; with the warmest heart, with the most expansive and hopeful philanthropy, with the most tolerant, most cheerful, most charitable love of man? Do we not all of us hold that, outside of this special, authoritative Written Revelation, thus promulgated, collateral with it, consistent with it, the creation of the same nature, there is another system still, a mental and moral nature, which we may with great propriety explore, and which we may very wisely and fitly study and enjoy? Into that system are we forbidden to pry, lest we become, or be in danger of becoming, Atheists, Deists, Pantheists, or Dilletanti, or Epicurean? What is there to hinder us from walking consistently with our faith and the preaching to which every Sunday we are so privileged to listen, — what is there to hinder us from walking on the shore of the great ocean of general truth, and gathering up here and there one of its pebbles, and listening here and there to the music of one of its shells? What is there

to hinder us from looking at that Natural Revelation that
shall be true hereafter? What is there in all this to prevent us in trying to open, if we can open, that clasped volume of that elder, if it may be that obscurer, Scripture?
What is there to hinder us from studying the science of the
stars, from going back with the geologist to the birthday of
a real creation, and thus tracing the line through the vestiges of a real and a true creation down to that later and great
period of time, when the morning stars sang together, exulting over this rising ball? What is there to hinder us, if we
dare to do it, from going down with chemists and physiologists to the very chambers of existence, and trying thence
to trace, if we may, the faint lines by which matter rose to
vitality, and vitality welled up first to animals, and then to
man? What is there to prevent us from trying to trace
the footsteps of God in history; from reading His law in the
policies of States, in the principles of morals, and in the
science of governments; His love in the happiness of all
the families of the human race, in animals, and in man;
His retributions in the judgments that are "abroad in all
the earth?" Is there anything to hinder us, in the faith we
hold, from indulging the implanted sense of beauty in tracing the last tracks of summer eve, or the first faint flush
that precedes or follows the glorious rising of the morning?
Because we happen to believe that a Written Revelation is
authoritative upon every man, and that there is contained
in it, distinctly and expressly, the expression of the need of
reconciliation, is there anything in all this, let me ask you,
my friends, which should hinder us from trying to explore
the spirit of Plato; from admiring the supremacy of mind,

which is at last the inspiration of the Almighty that gives you understanding, in such an intellect as that of Newton; from looking at the camp-fires, as they glitter on the plains of Troy; from standing on the battlements of Heaven with Milton; from standing by the side of Macbeth, sympathizing with, or at least appreciating something of the compunction and horror that followed the murder of his friend and host and king; from going out with old Lear, gray hair streaming, and throat choking, and heart bursting with a sense of filial ingratitude; from standing by the side of Othello, when he takes the life of all that he loves best in this world, "not for hate, but all for honor;" from admiring and saddening to see how the fond and deep and delicate spirit of Hamlet becomes oppressed and maddened by the terrible discovery, by the sense of duty not entirely clear, by the conflict of emotions, and by the shrinking dread of that life to come, as if he saw a hand we could not see, and heard a voice we could not hear? Certainly there can be no manner of doubt that our faith, such as you profess it and such as you hold it, will give direction, in one sense, to all our studies. There can be no doubt, in one sense and to a certain extent, that it baptizes and holds control over those studies; certainly, also, it may be admitted that it creates tendencies and tastes that may, a little less reluctantly, lead away a man from the contemplation of these subjects; but is it incompatible with them? Do you think that Agassiz, that Everett, — each transcendent in his own department of genius, — has become so because he held, or did not hold, a specific faith? Because you believe the Old Testament as well as the New, cannot you read a Classic in the last and best edition, if you know how to read it? That is the great question at last; and I apprehend that the incompatibility, of which we sometimes hear, has no foundation in the things that are to be compared. Did poor, rich Cowper think them incompatible one with another, when for so many years he soothed that burning brow, and stayed that fainting reason, and turned back those dark billows that threatened to overwhelm him, by his translation of the Iliad and Odyssey? What did he say of this incompatibility himself? "Learning has borne such fruit on all her branches; piety has found true friends in the friends of science; even prayer has flowed from lips wet with Castalian dews."

I hold, therefore — and I shall be excused by the friends of other denominations, now and here present, if I deliberately repeat and publicly record — that we have attended this Church, attached ourselves to this Congregation, and adhere to this form of Faith, because we believe it to be the old religion, the true religion, and the safest; and because, also, we have thought that there was no incompatibility between it and the largest and most generous mental culture and the widest philanthropy, that are necessary in order to complete the moral and mental development and accomplishment of man.

But there is another reason which I, — committing nobody, running the risk of differing from many of you, laymen and clergy, but assuming to act for nobody but myself, — with your permission, will proceed to give, as a reason why a sober, conscientious, and thoughtful layman might well have attended the Worship of this Church. And that is, permit me to say, that we have every one of us assuredly felt, as we came here from Sunday to Sunday and took our seats in our pews, that we should hear nothing in the world but Religion preached from that pulpit, and no manner of Politics, State or National, directly or indirectly. We came here, if we came as we professed we did, to hear of those things which pertain to religion, to the salvation of the soul, and to the rest everlasting. And I may be permitted to say for myself, that I have uniformly found it to be true, and I have uniformly reconciled, if I needed to reconcile, my own attendance upon this Church, by the consideration of that truth, — I have uniformly found it to be true that I heard nothing, was assailed by nothing, was secularized by nothing, was defended or attacked by nothing which I had done, nothing for which I had voted or acted in the political world without. All of us spent the week before, and all of us were obliged to spend the week afterwards, more or less in that same heated, heaving political world; there we acted, there we had to debate, there we lost our temper; but I thank my Pastor that I am able to say, in the presence of so many and such respectable clerical friends as these, as those I see about me, that never in an introductory prayer, never in a hymn, occasionally or in the ordinary course of public worship selected, never by any illustration in any sermon, by any train of association, right or wrong, was I carried back into the world that I had left, and which I should have been willing, for that day at least, to have forgotten forever. Of Religion, and a correct moral personal life, of these I came to hear, and of these alone have I ever heard at any time. I have no manner of doubt that there are a great many pulpits in Boston of which the same thing might be said. I do not personally know that it might not be said of every one. I know that it can be truly said of this, and I am thankful to be able to thus publicly state that I know it to be true.

And now, since I have mentioned this subject, my friends, may I be permitted, without presuming to complain of anybody, or to dictate to anybody, and still more, without assuming to myself to preach a *concio ad clerum*, or to preach at all, may I be permitted, on behalf of uninstructed and unprofessional laymen, to say one single word to serious clergymen on the duty of a rigorous abstinence from politics, and from any element which has been connected in any way with active party politics, on the Lord's Day. I need not say that I have a great deal too much personal respect and love for that profession in all its denominations, that I too perfectly appreciate the past and present transcendent good they have done to their country and to man, to wish, even if I had it in my power, to abate a tittle of the just respect that is due to them, or to impair in the least degree the just influence which they have acquired, and which they possess in this community, still less to intrude into that secret and elevated circle of private judgment which is every man's right. But I will say, I repeat, in behalf of laymen, once more, that it is exactly because we love and honor them,— it is exactly because we would do everything we can, not merely to pay the allotted salary, but everywhere to preserve to them the influence which the selection of their field of duty has entitled them to exert,— that I take the liberty, in the presence of some of them, to say something.

Permit me, then, to suggest, in the first place, that he

who preaches on Politics, or on any topic in the least degree connected with practical party Politics, in the pulpit, lays himself under the suspicion, at least from many, *many* laymen, that his motives are not entirely unobjectionable, and that thus he does something, or does much, to unfit him for the full and perfect performance of the great duty to which he has been solemnly called. I do not say that such a man is not a very bold man; I do not say that he is not a very sincere man; I do not say that he is not as bold and sincere as an old prophet standing up before a king, and, in the eloquence of an expiring nation, denouncing his sins and the sins of his people. But I mean to say that he runs a great risk of being suspected not to be bold and not to be sincere at all. He runs the risk of being suspected, and he is suspected, of denouncing a slaveholder, not because he hates the slaveholder or feels that he has anything to do with the business, but because some rich man in his congregation hates slaveholders, and because he pleases him by denouncing them. He runs the risk of being suspected, not of being brave against a danger which is a thousand miles away, but of being a coward and bowing down before a supposed danger that is very near him. He runs the risk of being suspected, not of being bold to challenge a man who cannot do him any harm, but of challenging that same man because he is afraid that another, who can do him harm, may be found within the reach of his voice. He runs the risk of being suspected, not of braving a danger that may arise from a distant region and a distant public sentiment, but of being afraid of a public sentiment at hand that may take the form of a danger, that may risk his salary, or, by possibility, induce the chance of calling a council of dismission. And thus it comes to pass, as I submit, and as I have heard it many times remarked, that this suspicion unfits him to do the duty which we expect of a minister of the Gospel; and thus of doing something to violate that great trust which he took upon himself with so much solemnity at his ordination, to let no man despise the ministry so far as he was concerned, and to preserve it for its proper influence in the noble specialty which has been assigned to it.

Permit me to give as a second reason, in the pursuit of this same course of thought, that intelligent persons, and very many intelligent persons, are too apt to think that the preacher of Politics in the pulpit really does not know his business, and that he is really above or below, or on one side of it, and does not understand his business. We listen to him, as we ought to listen, to the utmost extent of the Protestant theory of independent private judgment, when he interprets the Scriptures, when he teaches us morality; when he testifies of Eternal Providence, and "vindicates the ways of God to man;" when he teaches us that we are all sinners, that our natures are alike degraded, that the retributions of a common eternity are before us all. We listen to him with respect, and with nothing less than reverence; there his studies and his profession have fitted him for it; there he stands upon his own ground, and within his own charmed circle; there he is master, and we are his implicit disciples; for that exactly we prize, and for that exactly we pay him. But when he has left that ground, when he has taken up the occupation of Politics, is not his occupation wholly gone? Is not his power of instruction substantially gone? The great concrete of practical Politics, the workings of our special confederated system, the laws and conditions of our very artificial nationality, will he permit me to inquire whether or not his deep studies, *aliunde et diverso intuitu*, have enabled him to know anything at all of these? As an educated man, as a religious man, as a student of morals, he will know all about the obligations, origin, and general direction of the conscience. He will have learned from his Bible that the race of man is of kindred blood, — all of it; and he will have learned from his Bible, or from Nature, that all men stand on an equality of right and responsibility and duty before God. But how far these glorious generalities are modified and controlled by civil society of any description, which is also the work of God; how far these rays of light, as Burke beautifully expresses it, come to be refracted when they go into such a medium as this; how far history shapes all systems, and has shaped our system; how far, for example, the acquisition of a territory, — a new fact, — by the common blood and common treasure, makes it proper to lay it open to all, or shut it up against some; does he know aught of this? These things pertain to practical statesmanship, and he is no practical statesman, although he is better and holier and higher.

In saying this in the presence of clergymen, do I disparage the clergy? No more, my friends, you will agree with me, than the honest schoolmaster, who was himself a clergyman, disparaged Frederick the Great at the time when the whole world was ringing with his victories, by expressing a doubt whether, after all, His Majesty could conjugate a Greek verb in *mi* — exactly because it was not his specialty.

Suum cuique sua in arte credendum est. You remember how finely Goldsmith recognizes that rule in his "Retaliation." Speaking of Sir Joshua Reynolds, who stood at the head of his profession, the most tolerant, the most modest, the most inquiring of men, — and Goldsmith describes him as exhibiting that same character at the club, in society, everywhere; but he says that whenever any one who was conversing with him began to talk

> "Of their Raphaels, Correggios and stuff,
> He shifted his trumpet, and only took snuff."

Let me ask my clerical friends — again speaking for laymen — whether they think it to be quite fair play between man and man, to catch a parishioner in his pew, silent and still, by custom, decorum, and the manners of New England, and turn upon him every eye in the congregation for the politics he practises and for the party to which he has attached himself. Is it quite right — as a clerical friend now in my eye expressed it in a sermon some time ago, in every word of which it gives me pleasure to agree — that he should find himself suddenly plunged, as a man finds himself in a snow-bank, into a Caucus? I put it to you if it is fair, manly, moral, honest? Is it not cruel and cowardly so to treat an individual man? But while I hate and despise all manner of cant in Religion or in Politics, and while I do not think the *ad hominem* argument a very good method for the discovery of truth, in logic or out of it, let me, in the hearing of some of the clergy, venture to suggest that the preacher, of whatsoever faith, who thus overflows his banks upon any element connected, in the remotest degree, with the party considerations or organizations of the day, runs a great chance of hindering the salvation of that very soul which he has been ordained to promote and secure. They tell us, every one of them, that the salvation of the soul is the highest concern of man; they tell us, every one of them, that nothing on earth or in heaven can be compared with it, to the individual, in its consequences. There is sometimes upon their lips that tremendous expression,— whatever it means in the original,— "The redemption of their soul is precious, and it ceaseth forever." And yet do they not endanger that soul forever? The layman has no chance except on Sunday, and they rob him of that Sunday. Through the week, he has been anxious, busy, troubled; and he comes here on Sunday, as a man goes into his house at night-time, for rest and instruction. The Sunday is all he has, and you take away that Sunday; it is for you of that profession to say, it is for us to say on behalf of laymen, whether that is or is not consistent with the character of a preacher of Religion. Remember the very first word he hears in prayer, the very first word he hears in a hymn selected to be sung, however well it may be sung, and by whatever choir, the very first illustration in the sermon to which he may listen, sends him away gloomy and irritable, turns the whole service into a political mockery, and awakens a train of reflection that renders him, from first to last, inaccessible to the truth, closes his ear to the voice of the charmer, charm he never so wisely on that day. I repeat, then, Sunday is all that such a layman has, and the preacher of Politics has robbed him of that Sunday.

I do not know very well why I have fallen on this train

of thought, and it is high time to have done. Let us close as we began. Let us unite in the wish that our children and our children's children, when they come into this house on Sunday, may know as we have always known, and feel as we have always felt, that nothing but Religion will be heard from this pulpit; that nothing shall enter here that cannot enter and abide in that higher and better Temple of God, to which Religion points us, and to which Religion should conduct. Let us find, and our children and children's children find here, or in other houses of worship, exactly and merely this. Let us, as far as we may, avail ourselves of all the privileges which this Bethel affords; and if we fail to avail ourselves of those privileges and of the teachings of this pulpit, may that venerable and beloved Pastor be able to say, with his last words, as ever to us, " I am innocent of your blood."

A POEM was then recited by Reverend CHARLES C. BEAMAN, a former Member of this Church. The following extracts have been kindly furnished by Mr. B., at our request:

    HAIL to this hour! new strengthening from above
    The cherished flame of our fraternal love,
    And warm affection for a Pastor's care,
    Which all our hearts in pleasing union share.
    *   *   *   *   *   *   *

Lost Pleiads are restored to us to-night,
And stars new risen burst upon our sight;
Welcome we give to all who note this day,
Which marks one period in our Shepherd's way.

* * * * * *

The Installation hour! solemn and still,
Like the first pulses of a new-born rill,
Was birthplace of a stream, which, calm and deep,
And beautiful with many a winding sweep,
And flower-enamelled banks, with herbage green,
Rolls seaward still, as we so long have seen.

* * * * * *

And while these years have fled, how many things
Have touched the heart on all its sacred strings!
The first impression of our childhood's hour,
That linked our Pastor with a higher power;
Truths from his lips, persuasive to the soul,
Which made us turn and yield to God's control;
Instruction building up the work within,
And guarding us on every hand from sin;
With holy rites by him we have been bound;
He in our sorrow soothed the anguished wound.
Friend of our childhood, friend of riper years,
Companion in our Christian hopes and fears!
What tie more sacred binds the human heart?
What love less willing from the breast to part?

HYMN.

The following Hymn, by Miss LUCY E. SPEAR, a Member of the Church, was then sung: —

Come! let us with a cheerful voice,
    With joy, and praise, and song,
In this returning day rejoice,
    A happy, praising throng.
Come! let us bless that guardian Hand
    Which led us on our way,
And brought us, a united band,
    To gather here to-day.

Still at our head our Pastor stands;
    As Shepherd of the flock,
He guides us on through earthly lands,
    Still leads to Christ, our Rock.
In early youth, his lot was cast
    This pastoral charge to bear;
Now, five-and-twenty years are past,
    And we are still his care.

With us his manhood's toils are spent, —
   Toils by the Spirit crowned;
The fruits our gracious God hath sent,
   Behold them, all around;
While some, beyond the gates of death,
   A fairer bloom afford,
And perfume with their fragrant breath
   The garden of the Lord.

Still be our onward path pursued,
   And still new trophies won!
Still be the loving bonds renewed
   Which bind our hearts in one!
And long may he, whose works of love
   Our gratitude employ,
His faith and patience here approve;
   Then see his Master's joy.

Remarks by General Oliver.

REMARKS BY GENERAL OLIVER.

GENERAL HENRY K. OLIVER, of Lawrence, was next introduced as the Schoolmaster of Doctor ADAMS at the Latin School in Salem. He observed: —

That though, from the apparent coincidence of their respective ages, if judged by their respective personal appearances, doubts might be expressed about his being old enough to have been the instructor of the Reverend Gentleman, yet it was nevertheless true that he was so; for somewhere about the remote year of 1819, soon after graduating. He received an appointment in the School just named. And well do I remember (continued General Oliver) that when, stripling as I was, — not having then reached my nineteenth year, — I entered the school-room, well do I remember with what fear and trembling, and with what doubts, many and weighty, I cast my eyes upon and about the little "sea of upturned faces" and peeping eyes that greeted my entrance, and seemed to be weighing me in their balance. Well do I remember that my interpretation of the physiognomy of some of the one hundred lads before me presaged precious little comfort to my timid self. Had they known what boding anxiety and positive misgivings then possessed my soul, and worried out some "drops of dew" upon my youthful brow, — had the spirit of rebellious fun and naughty misrule lured them to the deed, as has sometimes happened when younglings from College are put in charge over younglings at School, — what an unequal contest might then and there have been waged. But my fears soon subsided, and left a welcome confidence in their place; for I perceived, to my great consolation, as I studied my new acquaintances, many a pleasant, many an honest, many an alluring face; and, among them all, (and how vividly does the scene return to my memory!) none more comforting and encouraging than the face of one quiet, sedate, unassuming, faithful, and confiding boy, now developed and matured into a noble manhood, in the justly beloved and venerated Pastor of this Church.

"Quantum mutatus ab illo!"

"How changed by passing years," yet only in the figure and the stature; for the boy of that early day was "the father of the man," and shadowed forth what manner of man he would be, should life and health be spared, and the promise of the days of his boyhood be thoroughly fulfilled, in the good Providence of God, in ripened years. And has not the ample accomplishment justified all the early hopes? Have I not a right to be proud that I had something to do in the developing and in the maturing of so goodly a fruit as this? May not a body be pardoned for believing, with so good a result as this before him, that his labors and his example were not of the poorest after all?

In those days of his school-boy life, with a persistent habit of patient study, with more than an ordinary memory, with an earnest and resolute spirit of research, he became a successful scholar, and ranked with the best of his associates. I well remember that, perceiving readily the spirit and meaning of the classic authors in the text-books then used, he seemed, at times, rather surprised that the other boys, as sometimes happened, shot rather wide of the mark. This was specially the case on a certain occasion, when one of his classmates, not quite grasping the intent and meaning of the great Roman orator in one of his imperishable orations, where he speaks of "*Statuas imaginesque avorum,*" (ancestral statues and images,) translated the words, "You place and you imagine your grandfathers," — (a rendering most certainly as far removed from the true one as you could reasonably ever expect to hear,) — his eyes dilated with amazement, as did mine; a quiet smile stole over his face, while the rest of us broke into a rather vociferous cachinnation, — the unlucky, blundering lad looking round with wonder, to see what had caused all this wild merriment.

Continuing his preparatory studies with constant success to their completion, in the fulness of his time he left School for the more trying scenes of a collegiate life. And here his efforts were sedulously continued, and crowned with the best results. So, too, in his further studies, directed more especially towards his preparation for the holy office which he has so faithfully and so happily filled, he was equally devoted; and now I see in the gentle lad, whom I used to call by the familiar household title of Nehemiah, the reverend, the learned Doctor of Divinity, beloved and respected wherever known, carrying a weight of character and a power of influence but seldom attained, and the earnest and successful Minister of Christ, winning souls into the kingdom of his Master, and faithfully discharging all the high obligations of the noblest profession that man can assume. I think all the better of myself and of my poor teachings, when I look on the two pictures they presented.

And now, my dear pupil of the days we never more shall see, let me thank you most heartily that in this the day of your well-deserved joy and reward, that in this the day of your gladness and festivity, you did not forget the teacher and guide of your earlier years, and that you desired his presence on so genial and interesting an occasion. God bless you and yours ever; and, when the jewels are made up, may you be among the brightest.

ODE.

The following ODE, by Mr. JONATHAN D. STEELE, (a former Member of the Church and Superintendent of the Sabbath School,) was then sung: —

THE CHURCH SILVER WEDDING.

Air, "Home, sweet home."

Though the world with its pleasures invites us to roam,
Why meet we to-night in this happy old Home?
For the Church and our Pastor each heart beats elate;
The Church Silver Wedding we now celebrate.
    Home, home, sweet, sweet home;
  'Tis sweet here to greet one another at home.

Age, manhood, fair maidens, sweet children are here;
Our absent ones send us their word of good cheer;
And wanderers returning rejoice to take part,
As Pilgrims they flock to this Mecca of heart.
    Home, home, sweet, sweet home;
  There's no place like home — the Church, our soul's home.

While we meet here together, remembrance imparts
Much sorrow and sadness, more joy, to our hearts;
The griefs we have suffered, the joys we have known,
These, Pastor and People have made all their own.
  Home, home, sweet, sweet home;
 All hearts throb in unison here at our home.

O Saviour! thy pastures have been to us sweet;
Still waters are these which have lain at our feet.
Feed, Saviour! thy people, still here, as of old. —
Be this Silver Wedding exchanged for the Gold.
  Home, home, sweet, sweet home;
 May Pastor and People long dwell here, at home.

Time! lay thy hand gently upon his loved brow!
Church, be thy name "Union," forever, as now;
When beckon'd above from this Union to come,
May Pastor and People be found still at home!
  Home, home, sweet, sweet home;
 Singing, Glory! Hosannah! in Heaven, our Home!

Remarks by the Pastor.

REMARKS BY THE PASTOR.

THE Pastor, being called upon, spoke as follows: —

Mr. Chairman, Respected and Dear Friends:

I had no expectation of what would befall me here when I agreed to be present. When it was first proposed by Deacon Scudder, a few months ago, that some notice should be taken of this Anniversary, I thought that it might be very useful for the Members of the Church to come together, and review the way in which God had led them, and me with them. Our friend said that he wished to have it more personal as regards myself; but I proposed to him, as the senior Deacon and the representative of the Church, that which Ahab proposed to Jehosaphat, — "I will disguise myself and enter into the battle; but put thou on thy robes." My desire was, that everything that should be said should have reference to the God of all grace, who has given me this happy ministry among this endeared people; but I did not think of being brought into such toils as I have found myself in to-night. The "toils" of the last twenty-five years are not to be compared with them.

As I witness these scenes, as I read the letters of congratulation which I have received, as I stand here to-night and look over these twenty-five years, I have had, and I have now, an idea of what I have supposed reminiscence might be in heaven; for I have often been visited with the thought, — how can we prevent the sad recollections of earth from interfering with the happiness of heaven? When I first thought of this occasion, to look back upon the past seemed sad; but, as I have approached it, I saw nothing but joy, and it has been to me a scene of unmingled joy. As I look back on the past, I feel as though I could now, and I wish that I could always, inscribe upon my breast that which is inscribed on a sun-dial in Spain: — "*Horas non numero nisi serenas.*" I count only the bright hours.

Why have I been here twenty-five years, and how has it so fallen out? Under the good Providence of God, one thing in particular has contributed to it in a measure. My brethren and friends in the ministry, I pray that it may be your lot always to have such Deacons as I have enjoyed here. Can I ask for you a greater blessing, as an aid to the Ministry of Reconciliation? This Church owes a debt of gratitude to those men, who have stood around me, and have been my counsellors and friends; discreet, kind, judicious men, — men who are not whimsical, and who are not continually troubling their Ministers with thoughts and fancies which are not of practical value. I owe them a debt of gratitude which I here wish to pay, "in the midst of thee, O Jerusalem." These men have been to me Aarons and Hurs, holding up my arms. I think, too, we owe a little, in the peace and prosperity which have attended us, to the circumstance, that our House of Worship has been in a measure sequestered. It has not been on the great thoroughfares of travel, and it has not been a matter of course that people should come to this place of worship. But, being a little removed from those thoroughfares, people have come here under the influence of affinities, and we have pursued our way without any interruption of harmony from the first.

I felt that it would not be suitable for me to say anything here to-night, and I was about to excuse myself; but I wish here to bear testimony to the uninterrupted kindness which I have experienced from this people, and which, to-day, has made me the recipient of blessings to which they have too much delicacy to refer,— and I have never known which to admire most, the generosity or the delicacy of this people, — blessings which, to-day, have confirmed by practical proof that which the twenty-third Psalm tells me, — " I shall not want." I forbear to say anything more about it; but I live among my own people, and I have a record in my memory of their goodness to me.

In conclusion, I have only to say that I have been reminded sometimes, when thinking of what has been called the retrogradation of stars, — some of whom never depart many degrees from the sun, but go down and then go back, — how happy it would be if we could all make that the emblem of our lives as Ministers of the Gospel; and, when we have gone down to a certain place, could rise again by retrogradation, so as never to be out of the Presence of the Great Luminary, that we might receive from Him the light which we desire to bestow upon others.

As I have spent the morning of a happy life with you, I shall be most happy, if it be agreeable to you, to spend the afternoon,—naturally having the desire, peculiar to old men, that I shall be allowed to go home before dark. I hope I may be so happy as to meet a multitude of this people gathered together who shall have been saved by my instrumentality, under God, so many of whom, thanks to His grace, now cast their crowns at his feet. Let me supplicate for each of us, my beloved brethren in the sacred office and pastoral life, a fulfilment in us of that inspired description of one who was an under-shepherd of God's Israel:—" So he fed them according to the integrity of his heart, and guided them by the skilfulness of his hands."

———◆———

Prayer was then offered by Reverend GEORGE W. BLAGDEN, D.D., of Boston.

The Benediction was pronounced by Reverend JOHN A. ALBRO, D.D., of Cambridge.

The Congregation were then invited to repair to the Lecture Room, where a Collation was in readiness. A blessing was invoked by Reverend JOHN C. STOCKBRIDGE, D.D., of the Charles Street Baptist Church. The social reunion here was highly gratifying to the numerous friends who were present.

Great credit is due to the Marshals and Ushers, by whose skilful arrangements and services the whole occasion proceeded with unexceptionable order, and to the great comfort and gratification of all concerned.

The Musical Services were conducted by EDWARD HAMILTON, Esquire, of Worcester, Chorister of the Society; by whom, also, the pieces were adapted and prepared for chanting.

On Tuesday afternoon, (the twenty-ninth,) the Church held another Conference Meeting in the Lecture Room, where the past and present Members of the Church made remarks, suggested by the great goodness of God in our past history, and encouraging and strengthening one another in their faith and hope.

As this was the closing public meeting of the Anniversary occasion, the past Members of the Church were addressed as follows by Deacon GEORGE ROGERS:

DEARLY BELOVED BRETHREN AND SISTERS:

With all our hearts we have welcomed you to our homes, and to the Church of our best love; to many of us the place of our spiritual birth, and to all the means of our growth in grace and knowledge of our Lord and Saviour Jesus Christ, through its appointed ministrations and ordinances, and also the scene of our most sacred and endeared associations. It has been a most blessed and happy reunion to both Pastor and People of Union Church. Solemn indeed has been the thought that nearly thirty-seven years have passed since its first organization, and twenty-five years since the Settlement of our present beloved Pastor, whose Anniversary occasions this reassembling. Yet we rejoice, because of these rich and abundant fruits of blessing.

We have, together, exchanged our congratulations; together have we bowed in prayer and praise to God our Saviour; together have we recounted our joys and griefs; together have we wept and rejoiced, in calling up the reminiscences of the past; and have almost, as if in rapt vision, seen hovering over us the spirits of our departed loved ones, — Pastor, Deacons, Husbands, Wives, Brothers and Sisters, Fathers, Mothers, Sons and Daughters, — among them, here and there, an infant "AGNES," but with no coffin "Key,"— alike mingling in these sacred scenes and hallowed remembrances.

Together also, again and again since our coming together, have we worshipped within these consecrated walls on the Sabbath; heard with rapt attention and swelling emotions the words of truth and grace, in sweet and touching tones and looks, from the lips of our dear Pastor; witnessed the simple and beautiful rite of Infant Baptism; received a new accession of brethren and sisters to membership in the Church; then communed with each other and our blessed Lord and Master at His own Table, in celebration of His Supper; and, lastly, we have beheld with admiring gratitude that large and intelligent audience of mental and moral worth, in the persons of Christian Pastors, Laymen, and friends assembled together, out of respect to the Pastor, at the commemorative exercises, listening with gratified delight and approval to the just and merited tributes of honor and affection paid to him by the orators of the occasion, in tones and strains almost as tender and eloquent as

> "Zion heard,
> When on his golden harp her Royal bard
> Waked to a glow devotion's dying flames."

And now, having once more mingled together our voices in prayer and hymns of praise, — listened to each other as we have given utterance to the emotions of our souls, — it is to me a delightful duty, in parting, to express to you, dear brethren and sisters, the sincere affection of our hearts, and the great happiness which this reunion has occasioned. Your faces have been to us a benediction; your cordial grasp of our hands, your smiles and tears and joys, have found an equally cordial response on our part. We thank you for your prayers for us and our dear ones, at our firesides where we have so lovingly knelt together. We have rejoiced to know that you still remember "Union Church;" you love her gates, her Pastor, her Doctrines, her Ordinances, and her ways; you still hold fast "to the faith once delivered to the saints," and glory in nothing "save in the cross of our Lord Jesus Christ." And we thank you for all those testimonials of attachment and kindness, to the Church and its Pastor, which your presence here at our invitation has evinced.

Take with you, then, dearly beloved, to your respective places of abode and the Churches of your present connection, the assurances that we love you still; that we are all one with you in Christ Jesus. Our prayers accompany you, that solid and unalloyed domestic and social enjoyments may ever be yours; that your dear children may all be gathered speedily into the fold of the Good Shepherd; that God may honor you with greatly increased fidelity and usefulness in his service; that you, we, and all dear to us as our own souls, may at last meet in the Kingdom of Heaven, welcomed by the Saviour himself. Beloved in the Lord! The night is far spent! The day is at hand! The morning light of the new Heavens and Earth, wherein dwelleth Righteousness, will soon break upon our glad vision! And, in anticipation of it, let me say,—not Farewell! but Good morning!

— ♦ —

In the evening of Tuesday, the Pastor received his Parishioners and former Members of the Church and Society at his house, where a season of social intercourse was enjoyed not soon to be forgotten. Aged Members of the Society, and invalids, who could not attend in the evening, were brought to the Pastor's house in the afternoon. The ages of five female members of the Church then present amounted to four hundred and seventeen years.

Notice was taken, at the gathering in the evening, of an appropriate token of regard made by the Young Men to Mr. PRESCOTT FISK, who has served the Society faithfully and acceptably as Sexton for nearly twenty-five years.

Mrs. ANN BURKE, of Cambridge, the only representative present of her grandfather, Deacon Nathan Parker, the first Deacon of the Church, and Mrs. DEBORAH HOWE, the only surviving Member of the original company of Church Members who first worshipped in the Essex Street Meeting House, were introduced by the Pastor.

This meeting under the Pastor's roof very appropriately concluded all the services held on this interesting and long to be remembered Anniversary. We have great cause for gratitude to God that He has permitted us to mingle in such scenes as these; and we humbly beseech Him, for His mercies' sake in Jesus Christ, to accept our humble efforts to honor Him and the ministry which he has established for our salvation.

The foregoing was prepared by a Committee, at the direction of the Church, as a Minute to be entered on its Records.

Correspondence.

CORRESPONDENCE.

THE Committee having in charge the preparation and printing of this Volume deem it proper to state, that the arrangement and printing of all its parts have been wholly under their direction, and that they have felt constrained to overrule the objections made by the Pastor to the printing of extracts from certain letters received by them, and a few by him, in reply to invitations. It will be borne in mind that this Volume is not published; it being for the use of the Society, and not for general circulation. We have felt that we and our children, and our successors in this Church and Society, have a claim to know and possess these kind and generous utterances of our contemporaries. The writers will excuse any seeming liberty which we have taken with their letters, when they know that copies of them are merely multiplied by the press for the eyes of those who will most fully appreciate and cherish their acceptable words.

We will furthermore state, that some of the minuteness with which we describe our doings in this Commemoration, is from a desire to perpetuate, in our recollections, even the subordinate things in an occasion which was, in every way, successful, and the source of hallowed pleasure.

EXTRACTS FROM LETTERS,

IN REPLY TO INVITATIONS, ETC.

From Joel Hawes, D.D., Hartford, Conn.

"Many pleasant remembrances of the Church and of the Pastor certainly engage me to be present on the occasion; were it not," &c.

"It seems but yesterday that I assisted in the Installation of your Pastor, by preaching the Sermon on that occasion. What changes! Your beloved Pastor can recall many more, relating to himself and the Church he has so long and so usefully served. My dear Brother GREEN, whom I loved with warm affection, your first Minister, he has gone to heaven I cannot doubt, and many loved Members of his Church, some of whom I personally knew and greatly esteemed."

From Brown Emerson, D.D., Salem.

"Your kind invitation suggests many pleasant reminiscences in relation to yourself and your beloved parents. The Lord, I doubt not, will enable you to bear with Christian humility the expressions of love and praise which will be poured upon you."

From R. S. Storrs, D.D., Braintree.

"May the same Spirit watch over you and preserve you in the same happy relations for *more* than twenty-five years to come, and crown your glorious ministry with ever-swelling triumphs of grace, to the conversion of thousands, who shall be your crown and your joy for ever in the Heavenly Kingdom.

"My pen is blunt and my thought obscure, but a heart as warm as flows in any bosom of those around you nestles within and pours forth the prayer, — Lord! bless the Pastor and the Flock of Essex Street in their mutual loves and labors, henceforth and forever."

From Enoch Pond, D.D., Bangor, Me.

"Our intercourse, during the early years of your ministry, was intimate, and to me exceedingly pleasant. I remember those Cambridge interviews with great satisfaction. I rejoice in your great usefulness, not only in Boston, but, by your publications, throughout the country."

From John Nelson, D.D., Leicester.

"My great respect for Doctor Adams, my interest in the Essex Street Church, and the uncommon attractions which the occasion promises, all conspire to make it a peculiarly hard piece of self-denial to decline the invitation. My hope and prayer is, that Doctor Adams, who has been continued in the Essex Street Church for a quarter of a century, rendering such eminent services not only to this Church but to the community at large, by his Christian deportment.

his scholarship, and his ability as a preacher and a writer, may long be continued in the same sphere of usefulness, and that the light reflected by him from the Sun of Righteousness, may shine still more broadly and brightly."

From Hon. Samuel Farrar, Andover.

"GENTLEMEN: ANDOVER, March 19, 1859.

"I have received, with great gratification, your invitation to participate in the Commemorative Anniversary of the settlement of the Reverend Doctor Adams as the Pastor of the Essex Street Church. I have great respect for your worthy Pastor. I do not know how much influence for good it might have had upon our Theological Seminary if he had not declined the appointment to the Bartlett Professorship of Sacred Rhetoric, to which he was elected by the Trustees in 1835. The infirmities of age, now in my eighty-sixth year, must forbid my complying with your very kind invitation. With great respect,

"Your friend and obedient servant,

"SAMUEL FARRAR."

From Richard H. Dana, Senior, Esquire, Boston.

"It is pleasant to be remembered on such an occasion as the Twenty-Fifth Anniversary of your Settlement. It takes me back to the years before that, when I went to Salem to call you to Cambridge. Then came our sociable drive to Andover, and Professor Stuart with his bowl of bread and milk, he professing to eat no meat, yet, every now and then, filching bits from the broad dish; next, the Ordination, and my Hymn, which the press criticised for my use of the word

'*Trine*,' but for which there is enough authority; and there were also your Andover and Cambridge Hymns, and the laying of the corner-stone, of a fair morning, which seems to be breaking upon me now, with Mr. Nathaniel Munroe's touching voice going up skyward through the leaved branches, and Deacon Hilliard, who fought the battle like a humble Christian and stout man, and our good friend ——, who would so often complain of the devil's tying him down in his chair when he should be up and at meeting,— which I never thought quite fair to lay upon the arch enemy, for you know that our friend had a heavy, sluggish frame,— but he was, doubtless, a sincere, humble, and tender Christian. Perhaps many of these words may seem light for the occasion; yet light words, you know, do not always come of light spirits, but rather are often the merry children of sad parents. You, while you may remember many short comings, have much to comfort you, in that, with God's grace helping, you have so labored and not in vain. My dear sir, if I ever set foot upon a platform, never should I more gladly do it than in an instance which concerns you so nearly. You will say to yourself, 'Well, it would be gratifying to me to see his face there; but it is just like him to keep away from such public meetings, and I know that he cares none the less for me though he is not coming now.'"

From Mark Tucker, D.D., Vernon, Conn.

"May your example of stability and earnestness be blessed to both ministers and people throughout the country. Allow me to present the following sentiment: 'The Essex Street Church, with its esteemed Pastor,—a tower of strength, a pyramid of light, a stable pillar of the Truth, — may they long stand together in the strength of God, and let their light shine and prove steadfast amidst abounding errors.'"

From Ralph Emerson, D.D., Newburyport.

"I know of no one whose jubilee I should more rejoice to attend than this of Doctor Adams. May he be spared in his usefulness among you to witness the more emphatic jubilee of half a century."

From L. F. Dimmick, D.D., Newburyport.

"My cordial congratulations that the Essex Street Church and Society have been permitted, for a quarter of a century, to enjoy the labors of so eminent and excellent a Pastor; and my congratulations to him, also, that he has been enabled to occupy his elevated station with so much credit to himself and so much usefulness to others."

From John Todd, D.D., Pittsfield.

"I hardly know of an occasion or a man whom I would take more pains to honor. It is said that, just before his death, Chancellor Kent said to his minister, the late Doctor Erskine Mason, that when he met with a minister who, in these days, could stay in the same place and occupy the same pulpit ten years, he was willing to take off his hat to him. The Chancellor would have to take off his hat two or three times to your minister, before he had met his own sense of propriety. There are no men who are perfect; very few that are admirable. I have never had the grace of humility sufficient to imitate any man, but if ever I obtain enough for the purpose, I know of no one whom I should be more likely to copy than Doctor Adams; for a star that can shine, year after year, unchanged and undimmed, only growing brighter and brighter, must be able to lead wiser men than I am to the place where the child Jesus is."

From Right Reverend Manton Eastburn, D.D., Boston.

"I fear that my engagements may deprive me of the pleasure of being present on this occasion, so solemn and interesting. If you will not consider me as taking too great a liberty, I will ask permission to take this opportunity of saying how much profit as well as pleasure I have derived from the occasional opportunities of intercourse with you which I have been permitted to enjoy; and how much satisfaction I have long felt in the fact that your able ministry in this city is one that uniformly presents the Lord Jesus, and adheres firmly, in a time-serving age, to those Scriptural truths, the preaching of which can alone secure the Spirit's blessing, and the reception of which in the heart is the only hope of man."

From Samuel Barrett, D.D., Boston.

"I was greatly pleased, and felt truly grateful, when I received your kind note inviting me to be present, this evening, at your twenty-fifth commemorative anniversary; and till this morning I have been thinking of the pleasure I should have in being with you. The allusion in your note to the comparative length of my ministry induced me to ascertain how I stand related, in this respect, to my brethren; and I have found, to my surprise, that, of all the settled clergymen in this city, (considerably more than one hundred,) no one has been for so many years as myself the sole pastor of a single parish."

From E. S. Gannett, D.D., Boston.

"My first thought on reading your note was, — why, certainly I shall go, and thank them with all my heart for inviting me; my second thought was, to answer the note at once. Something, however, prevented, and then I let my engagements, which were more than usual last week, take precedence of an acknowledgment that ought to have been made without delay. Will you accept this as the explanation of my silence, and as the only apology I can offer? And will you let me assure you that I shall attend this evening with the greatest pleasure, not 'as a senior pastor,' but as one who entertains feelings of sincere respect and regard for him whose anniversary will be commemorated. Difference of theological opinion has only given me the better opportunity to observe the integrity of his course and the genuineness of his faith, and no one who shall be there this evening will give more hearty consent to his professional and personal worth."

From G. W. Blagden, D.D., Boston.

"My Dear Brother:

"I also still feel the pressure of the Right Hand of Fellowship *you* gave *me* on the third of November, 1830, of which our old friend Doctor Beecher said, 'there never would be such another;' and I shall be happy in uniting with you and your friends in the interesting ceremonies."

From E. N. Kirk, D.D., Boston.

"Dear Brother Adams:

"Receive my fraternal congratulations on this semi-jubilatic Anniversary of your Pastorate. I fully expected to be with you last evening, and utter a word to swell the stream of kind feeling and of thanksgiving. But I had gone from a sick chamber to the pulpit on Sunday. The features of your ministry, which my feelings would have led me to make prominent, are the Scriptural character of your preaching; your bold, uncompromising, prominent presentation of the fundamental doctrines; the deeply-tender, evangelical, and practical tone of all your ministrations. There is a broad, deep line of demarcation between two styles of ministry, which, I fear, have not sufficiently attracted the notice of teachers in our schools of theological science. Some preachers aim to get religious truth into the soul through the avenue of Demonstration. The unobserved influence of their instructions is, to give their hearers unlimited confidence in their own reason as the medium of learning religion. The other class of preachers have become like little children, in order to enter the Kingdom of Heaven. Their motto is: 'I have believed, therefore have I spoken.' They have obtained all they know, not by speculation nor reasoning, but by believing. Their preaching nourishes faith. I thank God that you, my dear brother, are on this side of that great line.

"Be steadfast, immovable, always abounding in the work of the Lord.

"Yours, in sweet union of Christian fellowship," &c.

From Rev. H. M. Dexter, Boston.

"MY DEAR BROTHER:

"I so much regretted that the crowd last night prevented me from taking you by the hand to express to you my cordial interest in the scene, and my joy that one of our Pastors in Boston should be honored so deservedly for long and faithful service, that I cannot resist the impulse which I feel this morning to say thus much in this manner.

"Perhaps one situated as I am — in parochial circumstances wisely ordered by God's Providence to be very different from your own — has some keener appreciation of the joy and beauty of a thriving, prosperous, and united Church, passing on from decade to decade under the loved leadership of one honored Shepherd, than may naturally belong to those who have their perceptions less vivified by contrast. At any rate, I felt a special gladness last night for you, which would have found utterance from my lips if I could have reached your immediate presence. However much we may have differed, or may differ still upon questions that are collateral to our work, I should be doing violent injustice to the truth if I withheld from you the expression of my sympathy in your rejoicing, and of my heartfelt prayer that your people may enjoy your ministrations through a period which shall bring them and you to a 'Golden Wedding,' that shall only prelude, in its sweetness, the comfort of an eternal union before the throne of God and the Lamb.

"Your unworthy, yet affectionate brother," &c.

From Rev. A. C. Thompson, Roxbury.

"Dear Brother Adams:

"I give you joy to-day, — the twenty-fifth anniversary of your present pastorate. What tender and hallowed reminiscences are thronging upon your memory — reminiscences of parishioners now in heaven, of scenes in the sick room and the house of affliction; reminiscences of revivals, of sacramental joys, and of high delight in preaching Christ and him crucified. I have associated with you what Cranmer said of a minister whom he knew, '*Nihil appetit, nihil ardet, nihil somniat, nisi Jesum Christum;* and I cannot be mistaken in supposing that your chief joy to-day, in the retrospect of a quarter of a century, arises from having been an ambassador of the Lord Jesus Christ to the people of the Essex Street Church and Congregation.

"Sixteen years ago last July, you gave me the right hand of fellowship publicly and privately at the time of my ordination as Pastor of the Eliot Church. I had not been previously acquainted in person with any minister within fifty or a hundred miles of Boston. Your cordiality and kindness did much to make me feel at home at once, and from that time to the present there has been, outside of my own parish, no charm to make the region seem attractive, like the near presence and frequent meeting of dear Brother Adams. I am not aware that for these many years, I have once thought of the city of Boston without thinking of yourself. In regard to our meetings of ministerial and other associations, of the Prudential Committee and the like, one of my first thoughts has been, 'Will brother Adams be there?'

When you have been absent during summer vacations, it has seemed as if the city were out of town; and 'I had no rest in my spirit, because I found not Titus my brother.' How many times have I been to you for counsel, and never without being aided and refreshed! Your sympathy has been very precious to me, and it has shown itself in seasons of sorrow and of joy. You recollect it was said of Augustine and his friend Alippous, that they were *Sanguine Christi conglutinati.* A friendship so cemented subsists, I trust, between us.

"I need not tell you, dear brother, that my sympathies have gone out warmly toward you in the repeated and sore trials of these years, — trials domestic and public; while in the covenant blessings to your household, and in your successes as Pastor and author I have rejoiced, yea, and will rejoice. Your words and example have done much to incite and cheer me. God grant that my path may never lie far and long from yours.

"In that path be thou near me, and while I aspire,
Thou shalt calm all the thoughts that repine;
One in blood, in belief, one in hope and desire,
And the pinions that waft me are thine.

"In the desert that leads to the grave and its rest,
Is thy friendship a moistening shower;
In the tempests which life's rugged pathway molest,
Is that friendship a sheltering bower."

"Till our Lord shall come, and ever after,

"Your affectionate friend and brother," &c.

From Rev. Joseph Tracy, Boston.

" I still remember my connection with you as a precious privilege, and I have never yet been able to feel that it had wholly ceased. I send this testimony of my affection and respect for

" THE PASTOR, 'Who noble ends by noble means attains,' and who steadfastly refrains from using means that are not noble; never 'following a multitude,' nor suffering himself to be driven by a multitude, to 'do evil that good may come.' "

From Silas Aiken, D.D., Rutland, Vt.

" There is no one of my ministerial brethren with whom I have been on terms of greater intimacy, and taken sweeter counsel, and for whom I cherish a higher regard, than your beloved Pastor. The frequent and confiding intercourse of the twelve years that I was in Boston never knew an interruption. The service he has rendered to the cause of evangelical truth and piety, in your city and elsewhere, is of a value not easily computed. He has been a burning and a shining light, and long may the favor of Providence permit you to rejoice in his light."

From A. W. McClure, D.D., Quincy, Ill.

" Long and intimately as I have known him, there is no man living who stands higher in my love and reverence than your Pastor. There is no place this side of heaven where I could wish to be more than in your company, on 'the twenty-fifth anniversary of his settlement.' As I think of you on that joyful occasion, I shall feel as Bunyan did, when he saw 'the shining ones,' and 'wished himself among them.' If my severe ailments did not forbid it, I might well be there, as I am myself an Essex Street boy; for the old brick house in which I was born still stands at the corner of Essex and Kingston streets.

"May he live to celebrate the fiftieth anniversary of his settlement in Essex Street Church, amid just such proofs as he is now receiving of the unchanging confidence and affection of his people."

From E. L. Cleaveland, D.D., New Haven, Conn.

"It would give me pleasure to add my humble tribute of respect to that excellent man who has served you so long, so ably, and so faithfully in the Gospel of Jesus Christ. I honor Doctor Adams for the eminent example he presents of ministerial usefulness, of steadfast adherence to the faith, of wise and firm resistance to radical and dangerous innovation, and of patient forbearance under the stormy assault of popular excitement. The moral courage, the heroic spirit of a true Christian conservative in days like these, are worthy of special praise."

From Henry Wilkes, D.D., Montreal.

"Such is my high regard for Doctor Adams, and such my estimate of the Church and Congregation under his pastoral care, that, had I been within reasonable distance of your city, I should certainly have availed myself of your kindness."

From Austin Phelps, D.D., Andover.

"What a place that pulpit must be to you! The most of us must look up to you as a miracle of grace, in being kept so long in one line of pastoral service. I remember when I first saw you; you looked to me just as you do now. I cannot persuade myself that it is seventeen years ago, this week. I trust you have many years before you in that pulpit, and many souls that shall yet be given to you within those walls."

From the Same, to the Committee.

"I learned very early in my own ministry to esteem the fraternal offices of your Pastor, and I am still instructed by his writings. You do not need to be told of the multitudes who rejoice with you in the success of his labors, and with him in the appreciation of them by a grateful people. To many of us, it is like the shadow of a great rock in a weary land to see in the Essex Street pulpit a representative of permanence in the pastoral office in the City of Boston."

From W. G. T. Shedd, D.D., Andover.

"I beg to join my congratulations with those of the Christian public generally upon a union of such long continuance, and one that illustrates in such an eminent degree the worth of culture, character, and professional fidelity in the Pastor, and of affection and steadfastness in the People."

From Ray Palmer, D.D., Albany, N. Y.

"I united with Park Street Church during the great

revival of 1822-3, in the course of which I heard often the earnest and devoted GREEN, then Pastor of your Church. I knew some of its leading Members. I have rejoiced to know that you were among the most prosperous of the tribes of Israel. I have had a kind and fraternal acquaintance with your gifted, faithful, and widely-honored Pastor for many years. I should be glad to unite with you in thanksgiving for what he has been enabled to do for the Church at large while specially ministering to you."

From John Richards, D.D., Hanover, N. H.

" I send my congratulations to Doctor Adams for the Christian independence he has manifested in maintaining important principles amid a shower of public odium; and in drawing from Mr. Theodore Parker a public avowal of his sentiments, which cannot but redound to the best interests of true religion and the well-being of society." [The allusion here is to Mr. Parker's written avowal to Doctor Adams of the belief that Christ taught the doctrine of future endless punishment. See "Scriptural Argument," &c., by Doctor Adams, in the volume called " The Great Concern."]

From Rev. J. P. Gulliver, Norwich, Conn.

" Although my connection with it extended only over the period of my childhood, I retain vivid and delightful recollections of the Essex Street Church, and of those who were then connected with it. The countenance and voice of that most excellent man, the Reverend Samuel Green, are as fresh in my memory as though I had seen him yesterday. A very deep impression was made upon my mind by his appearance and words at the Communion Table; and I have often, in the course of my ministry, taken occasion to refer to the benefit I then received, as an argument to induce parents to permit their children to witness that ordinance. I remember, also, the vestry over the vestibule; the morning prayer-meetings, the Sabbath School, of which the late David Hall was Superintendent, and the meetings for inquiry, — all held in that room. I remember the meetings of the Maternal Association. The pleasant countenances and gentle words of those mothers left impressions that will never be effaced.

"Your present honored Pastor entered upon his work after I had left home to prepare for College. But his voice has been familiar to me from my earliest remembrance; and I can heartily enter into the spirit which prompts you to gather around him with so much affection and respect on this joyous occasion."

From Rev. Constantine Blodgett, Pawtucket, R. I.

"It would afford me great pleasure to be present, that I might testify my high personal regard for the Pastor, and my hearty approval of the conservative and Christian course of the Essex Street Church, over which he has so successfully presided."

From Rev. Erastus Maltby, Taunton.

"In these days of change, such an era in the ministry seems to demand some special recognition, and you do well in calling attention to that which, I fear, is fast becoming obsolete in our churches."

From Rev. Horace James, Worcester.

"May you add yet another twenty-five years to the sum of your ministerial labors. And especially may more such books of instruction and comfort as "Agnes and the Little Key," and "Bertha and her Baptism," fall from your pen, to quicken the faith of the Church respecting those themes, around which are clustered the hopes of the world."

From Rev. A. R. Baker, West Needham.

"I should gladly avail myself of an opportunity to show the respect which I feel for a church that has been steadfast in a relation to the same Pastor a quarter of a century, and that, too, in troublous times and in a place far famed as 'the city of notions,'— a respect second only to that which I feel for your Pastor himself, an able defender of the faith once delivered to the saints, who during this long period has stood up like a mountain of granite in a stormy sea."

From Rev. J. H. Means, Dorchester.

"Will you permit me most heartily to congratulate you on the occasion. The earliest sermon which I can distinctly remember was one which you preached at the Old South when I was quite a boy, and I think I may add that the few other sermons of yours which I have been permitted to hear have each left a definite impression.

"May your semi-jubilee so cheer you, that you shall gird yourself with new strength for the many years of usefulness which I trust remain."

From George W. Hosmer, D.D., (College Classmate,) Buffalo, N. Y.

"Dear Classmate:

"I should very much enjoy being near you in hours so full of interest to you. Please accept my cordial sympathy with the spirit that prompts you to remember your Classmates in the great days of your life. I am happy that you have so much to remember and to enjoy in the success and usefulness of your life."

From Cazneau Palfrey, D.D., (College Classmate,) Belfast, Me.

"I heartily congratulate you on all the happy circumstances of such an interesting occasion. To have been permitted to dwell for a quarter of a century among the same people, is a privilege and blessing that can be appreciated only by one whom Providence has led through frequent changes. My last letter to you was dated from Cambridge, and addressed to Andover. The interval covers the main portion of our actual lives. Ever truly your friend and brother," &c.

From William M. Russell, M.D., (College Classmate,) Barre.

"Dear Classmate:

"In these days of change, free-thinking, and radicalism, it is a great success to be able to commemorate a settlement over a people in the character of a Gospel Minister of a quarter of a century. To be able to achieve such a success, one must have some sterling qualities of virtue and character, something more than mere rhetorical display; some

Christian, life-inspiring goodness, that rises above and lives down political strifes and religious controversies.

"Although my views of Christianity differ from those held by the popular sect, I cannot shut my eyes to personal worth, nor withhold the meed of praise due to devotion to the cause of our common Redeemer, to faithfulness in one's calling, and to consistency in holding to one's convictions of truth and right."

From William H. Fowle, A. M., (College Classmate,) Alexandria, D. C.

"I do not know when I have been more gratified than at the receipt, a few days ago, of a 'Classmate Ticket' to the commemoration of your Twenty-Fifth Anniversary. Your labors in the cause of Christ have not been unnoticed by me, and, though not a member of the same communion, not unappreciated. Yours, in the bonds of Christian love," &c.

From Rev. Robert Southgate, (Andover Classmate,) Ipswich.

"It would give me great pleasure to attend, both because of the interest connected with the exercises of the occasion, and also because of my high regard for Doctor Adams as an old-time classmate in theological study, and a true champion in the ministry since, for the truth of God."

From Rev. Caleb Kimball, (Andover Classmate — now for many years blind,) Medway.

"It would afford me peculiar gratification to be present at your contemplated social gathering, and look back with you upon all the way in which God in his merciful and gracious Providence has led you for a quarter of a century. It is certainly a matter of devout thanksgiving that your life and health have been spared so long amidst such varied and exhausting labors; and that, during a period when ministers have been often compelled to change their fields of labor, you have been able to sustain so long, and with so much ability and success, your present pastorate. The study and labor it has cost you, and the anxieties experienced in being the successor of such a holy man and able preacher as Reverend Samuel Green, are fully known only to yourself. What a vast amount of truth has been communicated in the twenty-five hundred sermons preached to your people during your ministry! How many souls led to Christ! How important and various the instructions communicated at weekly meetings, in pastoral labors, and in visits to the sick and the dying. I rejoice, too, in the uniform harmony and friendly feeling which has ever existed between you and your people; in their high appreciation of your ministerial services; in the ample support so cheerfully given, and in the large amount contributed by them to send that precious Gospel, which they so highly prize, to the dark and destitute portions of the world. These are some of the considerations which will cluster around and render the meeting a joyful occasion.

"Although I am sightless, and have been unable to read for upwards of thirty years, allow me to say that I have heard read with pleasure and profit most of your printed sermons; and, were I able, would gladly possess and peruse every printed page which has proceeded from your pen.

"On account of feeble health, with which I have been

afflicted for four years, I shall be unable to be present at the meeting in prospect; but I hope to spend a portion of the day and evening in prayer to God that the services of the occasion may leave a deep and lasting impression on the minds of all who may enjoy them."

From Rev. Martin M. Post, (Andover Classmate,) Logansport, Indiana.

"Forbidden to be present, I am, in sympathy, with the projected occasion, and could very heartily partake of testimonies of honor and esteem to Doctor Adams, and of thankfulness to God for continuing him with you so many years, and with eminent advantage not only to the Essex Street Society and to Boston, but also to the interests of Christ's Kingdom throughout the world.

"Thirty years ago, well nigh, we sung at Andover our 'Parting Hymn,' an offering of Brother Adams's Muse. Since then, my position of a pioneer, where I now am, remote, has allowed me very rarely a glimpse of my old Classmate's person. But I have been a gratified observer of that chaste and benignant influence, and that substantial usefulness, steadily growing and ripening, of which the early elements of his character gave promise.

"Long may He who walketh in the midst of the golden candlesticks, and holdeth the stars of the Churches in His right hand, preserve to you the light of your beloved Pastor, even as one who turns many to righteousness, and shall shine as the stars for ever and ever."

From Rev. S. H. Keeler, (Andover Classmate,) Calais, Me.

"It is the Anniversary not only of a Classmate but of one for whom I have ever cherished the highest esteem and the most fraternal regard. Cordially do I bless God, and congratulate both you and your people, my brother, in view of your protracted and successful ministry with your present charge. Yours has been a responsible post, and well has the grace of God enabled you to fill it."

From William Adams, D.D., New York.

"Compelled by special engagements to remain at home, I cannot forbear saying a word by way of expressing my admiration of your career in the Christian ministry. Our acquaintance began in the Seminary. Your influence over me, by your fine taste and gentle ways, began when I first heard you speak. We were afterwards settled near each other. In affliction, I was 'before you.' I have admired your course, and feel greatly indebted to your example and your pen. You have had special trials of feeling within a few years past, not the less severe because undeserved. You will not only survive the aspersions of the unkind and the fanatical, but will deserve a larger honor because of them. Pardon me if I quote, in this connection, the words of Robert Hall : ' Distinguished merit will always rise superior to opposition, and draw lustre from reproach. The vapors which gather round the rising sun, and follow it in its course, seldom fail at the close of it to form a magnificent theatre for its reception, and to invest with variegated tints and with a softened effulgence the luminary which they cannot hide.'"

From William A. Stearns, D.D., President of Amherst College.

"What memories will this, your twenty-fifth anniversary recall!—how many happy scenes and events—how many sad hours of bereavement and loneliness, and of official and personal trials. Many, many who were interested in your settlement have passed away;—brethren and fathers in the ministry, fellow communicants at the table of Christ, respected associates and dear old friends gone,—forever gone. You have had your trials, my brother, but after all few men in the ministry have been so greatly blessed. God has signally crowned your endeavors and given you decided success. Now, though none of us have any thing but Christ to glory in, I do rejoice that he has made use of your agency, by your preaching, and your books, in converting sinners and greatly edifying the Church. It *is* a glorious work, this of the ministry. No employment on earth can compare with it. I trust God will give you yet many years to serve him in it; and though with you, as with me, the sun has crossed the meridian, it is my prayer for you that it may have a long and cloudless afternoon, and a glorious going down."

It is consonant with the general tone of the Anniversary Exercises that the highly esteemed "SCHOOLMASTER," who added so much to their interest, should now be heard, on " review."

From Hon. H. K. Oliver, Lawrence.

"MAYOR'S OFFICE, Lawrence, April 5th, 1859.

"REV. N. ADAMS. D.D., Boston :

"My Dear Sir, — Your very kind and gratifying note of the 2d inst. is at hand, and I thank you very earnestly and sincerely for its hearty tone and reciprocity. I assure you that I felt truly delighted that I was remembered by you in connection with your 'silver ceremonial,' and that I was privileged to be with you and your friends. Had I had a premonition of being called upon to say anything, I could have — as I have since done — recalled several interesting reminiscences connected with your boyhood and school-life. Your good chairman caught me '*non paratum*,' and I felt awkward and confused. But if you and your friends are satisfied — *si tu et amici tui contenti sitis, ego non minus.*

"This matter of love and of friendship, — I mean when they are full of life and of vigor, — when they are of that sort that time neither wilts nor weakens, — that worldly interests do not chill — '*perpetuâ viventes juventâ.*' — that flourish in undying youth — that dilate the heart whenever the eye of the body catches a glance of the friend's face, or the eye of the mind recalls his absent features and form, — this matter of love and of friendship, of such sort, has always seemed to possess a sort of celestial origin and to be a spark of the divine mind kindling the dull fires and waking the '*sopitos cineres*' of our poor mortality. I have always, from earliest boyhood, felt a yearning towards sympathetic and congenial hearts, and some few such I have enjoyed. Yet over most of them the grave has closed, though, thank God, with but a feeble bolt, which the first blast of the angel's trump of summons shall tear open, as it were but of straw. These men, the love of the world and the desire, the greed of gain, had not solidified. Though here, and of earth, their hopes, their aspirations, their certain and immutable faith were beyond earth, and in Heaven. With them, friendship was, as says Cicero, '*Non de vulgari aut de mediocri — sed de verá et perfectá qualis est eorum, qui pauci nominantur, fuit. Secundas res splendidiores, et adversas leviores, facit talis amicitia.*'

"Among these loved men, it has been a great satisfaction to me, to find those who, in their boyhood, were my pupils. For it is a good testimony in my behalf, that my instruction and my intercourse with them profited both head and heart. You, and R******, and B******, and K***, and C******, *et multi alii*, were such, and as I meet them in the whirr and whirl of the world, a gleam of sunshine and of comfort darts through the cloud under which I have very often journeyed and do now journey. This sort of feeling, first springing up in youth, when the heart is tender and warm, — for age generates no permanent loves, — keeps us young and sympathetic, and ready with deed and word to serve a friend, — '*bonâ spe prælucet in posterum, nec debilitari animos aut cadere patitur.*' You see that some vestiges of Cicero's beautiful treatise, ' De Amicitia,' still linger in my memory and drop from my pen. But where am I? The last page is reached and I must close. God bless us both, pardon our offences, (are they not many?) and permit us an unbroken friendship here, to be enlarged, purified, and 'of all earthly drossness quit,' and rendered immeasurably and eternally holy in His own kingdom beyond the tomb.

"*Sic vult et sic precatur, amicus tuus adhuc, ut antehac, et posthac in secula seculorum.* H. K. OLIVER."

The Pastor has seen fit to insist, in his turn, upon overruling the Committee; and he takes the responsibility, while we insert, at his direction, the following letters:

"BOSTON, March 27th, 1859.

"REVEREND NEHEMIAH ADAMS, D.D.:

"Dear Sir,—In the name and on the behalf of numerous friends of your Church and Society, who desire to improve the present interesting occasion of the commemoration of the Twenty-Fifth Anniversary of your Settlement as our Pastor and Teacher, to bear testimony to the faithfulness of your ministerial labors, to the firmness and consistency of your character as a Minister and a man, and to assure you of our appreciation of your untiring labors for the spiritual benefit of ourselves and our families, and as a token of our affection, and a pledge of our support and aid, in all your efforts for the advancement of Christ's Kingdom on the earth,— we ask your acceptance of the inclosed check for eighteen hundred dollars.

"Most affectionately yours in our Lord Jesus Christ,

"CHARLES SCUDDER,

"In behalf of himself and other Contributors."

"BOSTON, March 26th, 1859.

"DEAR SIR:

"By the bearer of this note I send you a new Seven-Octave Piano, which I shall be pleased to have you accept in place of your old Six Octave which you now have, if an exchange will be agreeable to you. And if the additional strings of the *new scale*, as they vibrate, shall add one note of joy and pleasure to your heart, may you also be reminded of the grateful love and esteem of myself and family to you, as a kind friend and faithful Pastor.

"That the only discord among us may be a discord of metal strings, which will only need a little tightening occasionally, is the sincere prayer of your friend,

"GEORGE H. DAVIS."

The importance and difficulty of the subject of *Sacred Music*, in connection with the affairs of a Religious Society, justify the insertion, here, of the following letter:

From Edward Hamilton, Esquire, Worcester, for several years Conductor of the Singing at Essex Street Church.

"Worcester, March 29th, 1859.

"Reverend Doctor Adams:

"Dear Sir,—Indispensable business engagements at home will deprive me of the pleasure of meeting you at your house, with your parishioners, this evening. It is a most welcome duty to acknowledge the receipt of the kind note with which you have favored me, and to express to you, in return, a grateful sense of the uniform courtesy and kindness which you have so unremittingly extended to me during the eight years of my connection with the Essex Street Society. Without making invidious comparisons, I must be allowed to say that never, during a service, in similar relations, extending over a period of nearly twenty-seven years, have I been so uniformly happy in respect to my intercourse with the Pastor. For the first time, I have found the dignity and importance of sacred music appreciated, as, in my judgment, it deserves to be; and it is greatly to be desired that this were, elsewhere, more generally the case. When, after a solemn chant by the choir, the clergyman rises and invites the people to commence the worship of God, I feel as if the office of praise was undervalued, and that, in *that* Society at least, it would not be likely to become a means of edification to the worshipping assembly, however brilliant and skilful, as an artistic performance, it might happen to be. I have often, in other places, had reason to regret this indifference on the part of the Minister, but never, I am happy to say, at Essex Street.

"For your unwearied efforts to assist me, in every way in your power, to know the tastes and wishes of the people; for your ever friendly and candid communication of your own preferences, made without any of that spirit of dictation which might, perchance, sometimes wound the self-love of the leader of the choir; and for your constant care to save me unnecessary trouble and embarrassment, by sudden changes in plan and purpose, I cannot sufficiently thank you. I will only add, that the years passed at Essex Street have been as free from the annoyances peculiar to the conductor's office, as any other years of my life. And I am happy to testify, that, if the path has not been altogether one of roses, it is not because you, my dear sir, have failed to strew goodly flowers of courtesy and kindness, in generous profusion, in the way.

"The members of the choir, as well as myself, leave the Essex Street Church, and especially its Pastor, with many regrets. And be assured, sir, that your approbation, so freely and fully bestowed, will go far to allay any apprehensions which, upon a review of all our acts in this relation, might arise, lest we may, at some times, have come short of our whole duty, as leaders of the praises of the sanctuary.

"With cordial respect and esteem, I subscribe myself, most truly, your obliged and grateful servant,

"EDWARD HAMILTON."

A SILVER FLOWER VASE, from the Young Ladies of Essex Street Society, which, we know, excited admiration and gratitude in the recipient, is the appropriate receptacle of frequent tributes which gladden the Pastor's Study.

Brief History of the Church.

BRIEF HISTORY

OF THE

UNION CHURCH,

IN ESSEX STREET, BOSTON, ITS FIRST PASTOR AND DEACONS.

———•———

IN January, 1819, a Congregational Church was gathered in Boylston Hall, under the pastoral care of Reverend James Sabine.

Individuals among them, — of whom Deacon Nathan Parker and Deacon James Melledge bore the principal part of the expense, with help from others, — erected the Meeting-House in Essex Street, which was dedicated in December, 1819. The Church took the name of "*Essex Street Church.*"

Two years after, difficulties arose between the Pastor and some of the Church, which resulted in the withdrawal of the Pastor with the Church as a body to Boylston Hall. A minority continued to worship in the Essex Street Meeting-House, — the premises being the property of individuals, and chiefly of those who remained.

On the twenty-eighth of March, 1822, they requested dismission from the Church in Boylston Hall, and, on the tenth of June, 1822, they were organized as a separate Church by an Ecclesiastical Council. They soon made application to the Old South and Park Street Churches for a contribution of Members. Nine brethren — three of them with their wives — were accordingly deputed from those Churches to strengthen this young Church. An inspection of their names will satisfy those who remember these men, that no Church ever had a more intelligent and efficient band of brethren in its beginning. To mark this fraternal and happy transaction, in which the three Churches were thus engaged, the name of UNION CHURCH was adopted.

ORIGINAL MEMBERS OF UNION CHURCH.

FROM THE ESSEX STREET CHURCH, (BOYLSTON HALL.)

Deacon Nathan Parker,
" James Melledge,
Joseph Noyes,
Joseph Morton,
Marquis F. Joscelyn,
Mrs. Eunice Joscelyn,
Mrs. Mary Ann Howe,
Mrs. Catharine Thayer,
Miss Mary Ann Howe,
Miss Martha Howe.

FROM HALIFAX, MASS.

Mr. Marcus Howe,
Mrs. Deborah A. Howe.

The following Members, already referred to, were dismissed from their respective Churches to strengthen this Church, and they were received August twenty-sixth, 1822, namely: —

FROM THE CHURCH IN BRAINTREE.

Deacon Josiah Vinton.

FROM THE OLD SOUTH CHURCH, BOSTON.

Deacon John Gulliver,
Mrs. Sarah P. Gulliver,
John Stimson.

FROM PARK STREET CHURCH, BOSTON.

Andrew Bradshaw,
Aaron Woodman,
John W. Rogers,
Mrs. Martha Rogers,
Daniel Noyes,
Gilman Prichard,
David Hale, Jr.,
Laura Hale,
Ezra Haskell.

REVEREND SAMUEL GREEN,

FIRST PASTOR OF UNION CHURCH.

On the twenty-sixth of March, 1823, God bestowed upon the Church a great blessing, in sending them the Reverend SAMUEL GREEN, then Pastor of the First Church in Reading, Mass., to be their Pastor.

Of this most excellent man, whose memory is so justly dear to many of us, it were difficult to speak in terms of love and praise which would surpass his merits as an able and faithful man of God. His presence was commanding, yet conciliatory; his face combined intelligence, firmness, and love; he had unction in his delivery; he was thoroughly imbued with the principles of theology as taught in the Westminster Assembly's Catechism. There was such sincerity and earnestness in his presentation of the Gospel, that many who did not relish the truths preached by him, were persuaded when he reasoned with them out of the Scriptures; so that he drew from the ranks of error those whose intelligence, cultivation, and wealth, made them chief pillars in our Evangelical Churches.

He was born in Stoneham, Mass. He was graduated at Harvard College, in 1816. He took a deep interest in a controversy which arose with regard to the Hollis Professorship of Divinity at Harvard College, and wrote

a series of articles in the Boston Recorder, under the signature of "Hollis," which were afterwards gathered into a pamphlet. He also wrote some useful tracts for the American Tract Society, among which was one called "One Hundred Arguments in favor of the Supreme Divinity of our Lord Jesus Christ."

Mr. Green labored here from March, 1822, till 1831, when his health failed, in consequence of his exertions during a season of great religious interest. He was released from active duty, and spent some time in Europe; but the inroads of disease upon his constitution were not abated, and his connection with his people was terminated, at his request, March twenty-sixth, 1834, by the Council which installed the present Pastor. To this Church, and to the city and its vicinity, he was most truly a burning and a shining light.

During his ministry of eleven years, (including the three years of his sickness and absence, in which many who were the fruit of his sowing were gathered,) there were added to this Church,

On Profession of Faith . . .	423
By Letter	177
Total	600

He died November twentieth, 1834. The present Pastor says: "Never did I select a text which seemed to me at the time, or which has since appeared to me more completely adapted to the subject, than the text of the Sermon which I was requested to preach at his funeral: '*For he was a good man, and full of the Holy Ghost and of faith; and much people was added unto the Lord.*' The day before he died, he took my hand, and, in a way which can never fade from my memory, he said: 'The blessing of the everlasting God be on you and on your people.'"

———◆———

DEACON NATHAN PARKER.

NATHAN PARKER, one of the first two Deacons of this Church, and by whose munificence chiefly this house was built, was born in Malden, Mass., 1754. He died in Dorchester, Mass., August eighteenth, 1830, aged seventy-six. He was one of twelve children. He was in the Lexington battle, being then not far from twenty-one years of age. He was also present and assisted at the "Tea Party," in Boston Harbor. This is confirmed by several living witnesses, who heard him relate it. He went to St. Johns, Newfoundland, and there became successful in business and accumulated property. With his friend and partner in business, Deacon Melledge, he went into the woods and cut the timber for a House of Worship,* which was occupied by the First Calvinist Church in St. Johns, and during his life he was instru-

---

* "The two elders erected it in twenty-eight days." — *Sketch of the Hist. of Cong. in St. Johns, Newf., by the Rev. George Schofield,* p. 6.

mental in building at least twelve meeting-houses, he being in every case the largest contributor. He had seven children, six sons and a daughter. Two of his sons were ministers of the Gospel, Reverend David Parker, formerly settled at Rhinebeck, New York, and Reverend Silas Parker, formerly of Mansfield, O. Both have deceased. They were educated at Yale College. Reverend David Parker went to England, where he married the daughter of the excellent Reverend Doctor Bogue, with whom he and Reverend Doctor Codman of Dorchester for some time studied theology. Mrs. Parker, (daughter of Doctor Bogue), survives, and now lives near Liverpool. Only one child of Deacon Parker is now living, — Judge Jacob Parker, of Ohio.

The wife of Deacon Parker died in Newfoundland in 1797. An account of her is found in the London Evangelical Magazine for that year, written by her Pastor, who says, "The subject of the following lines is Mrs. Ann Parker, late wife of Nathan Parker, who has been to me a faithful and judicious friend and fellow-sufferer in all my reproaches for Christ." She admonished her children, in her last hours, of their obligations to love and serve God in view of their having such a father, "whose instructions," she said, "have been so good and his example so proper."

His ancestors left England during the reign of Charles I., "to seek in America liberty of conscience and freedom in worshipping God. He preserved in himself all the sentiments and principles, with very much of the manner, of the Pilgrim Fathers."

He was a man of unbounded kindness and liberality, whose purity and sincerity were evinced by remarkable acts towards his own immediate kindred, when there was no room for ostentation nor publicity.

With his friend, Deacon Melledge, he removed to Boston, and they lived near each other for many years, in Charles street. He was at one time Deacon of Park Street Church. The cause of evangelical religion in this city seeming to require another place for public worship, Deacon Parker contributed about thirty-three thousand dollars towards the erection of this house.

Deacon Parker and Deacon Melledge now sleep together in the same tomb, in the cemetery under Park Street Church.

ANNA, the only daughter of Deacon Parker, married Samuel Bulley, of Teignmouth, Devonshire, and after her marriage went to England with her husband, who died there. In 1819 she left England with her children to comfort her aged father in his last years. She joined this Church in 1823, and died in Boston, March twenty-seventh, 1824. She left three daughters and one son, the eldest child, Lucy, having died at the age of seven.

MISS ANNA BULLEY, her second child, now deceased, occupies an honorable and most interesting place among the past members of our Church. Her mother died when Anna was seventeen years of age, leaving to her care four younger children, and their grandfather, Deacon Parker, then advanced in years and infirm. She joined this Church in March 1824, at which time, it will be seen by referring to the list, the Church received other valuable and important accessions. She died at the house of Reverend Doctor Codman, in Dorchester, October sixteenth, 1828, at the age of twenty-one. Doctor Codman published a brief account of her. The beautiful history of her life was written and published in England in 1851, entitled, " Anna, The Elder Sister."

Doctor Codman says of her, " Miss B. was remarkable for intellect, temper, piety, and personal appearance. Her understanding was singularly clear and even masculine; she had a mind capable of any efforts; she was distinguished for sound judgment, and I hesitate not to say that there is not, for discretion and propriety, an individual in my own congregation that I would sooner have consulted in a case of difficulty than Anna B."

The following extract from one of her letters will give the reader further information and good impressions respecting her grandfather, Deacon Parker:

" Dear grandfather has had a good deal of suffering; through much of it he was insensible, and I confess I had not the smallest hope of his recovery. The other evening he called me to him, and said, ' Anna, I have lost much strength and I am declining in health very fast. I may be called suddenly away from time to eternity. It devolves upon you, as the oldest of your family, to sustain the honor of religion in it. I trust you will be an ornament to it; may you grow in grace, my dear child, and may God bless you more and more. I trust you will ever walk in the faith of my fathers uncorrupted, believing in the blessed doctrines of the Divinity of Christ, and his atonement; keeping holy the Sabbath, and adopting that system of faith contained in the excellent Assembly's Catechism. My ancestors have, most of them, been men distinguished for piety, and out of respect to them I should have wished to have lain by their side, and been buried in the sepulchres of my fathers; but, owing to the errors which have crept into the church and town of M——, and the present unsettled state of religion among them, I rather wish to be buried in Boston, by the side of your mother. As to my temporal affairs, I leave them without anxiety; they are, I believe, arranged as far as possible.'" *

———•———

DEACON JAMES MELLEDGE.

He was born in South Street, in this city, in the year 1767, and died in Boston, January twenty-ninth, 1844. When he was eight or nine years old, at the beginning of the Revolution, he was sent to live with his relatives

* The representative of Deacon Parker has presented his cane to be the property of the Senior Deacon of this Church for the time being. Two sons of two deacons in our Boston Churches bear his family name with theirs, viz. NATHANIEL P. WILLIS, and JAMES P. MELLEDGE.

in Newfoundland, where his good behavior, industry, and integrity won the esteem of his employers, till at length he was taken into partnership. He was greatly prospered in business.

He and Deacon Parker were instrumental in establishing an Evangelical Church in St. Johns. It has already been stated that they went into the woods, cut the timber, and with the aid of others, built a small place of worship. A converted soldier was their first religious teacher.* They maintained a prayer-meeting at five o'clock in the morning. During their efforts to build up their society, they suffered much opposition. Coming to Boston, in 1818, he brought with him the experience and the habits which had made him useful as a Christian in the Provinces. He contributed largely for the erection of this place of worship. Deacon Parker and he were the first deacons of this Church.

If any man loved Christ supremely and ardently, it was our friend. The mention of the Saviour's name in ordinary conversation would frequently excite emotions in him which failed of utterance. Those Sermons interested and affected him most which exalted Christ. Frequently, after the Sabbath, when Christ had been the special subject of discourse, he has grasped the Pastor's hand with both of his, and while the tears ran down, he would say, "You will hear from these Sermons; the

* The Rev. John Jones, of Wales. — *Schofield's Sketch, &c.*

people cannot resist such a Saviour; 'He is chiefest among ten thousand; He is altogether lovely.'"

He looked upon himself as nothing; for the more we exalt the grace of God, the more we sink in our own esteem. His confidence and joy in Christ, therefore, did not awaken spiritual pride. Such was his sense of insufficiency, with regard to his feelings toward Christ compared with the Saviour's character and love, that he sometimes feared he did not love Him, so that in the days of weakness, when asked if he enjoyed the presence of Christ, he would uniformly answer, with every sign of deep humility, "Yes, I trust that I can say, Lord, thou knowest all things, thou knowest that I wish to love thee." He had a strong sense of the Saviour's personality. He loved to pray to Him. His power of speech failed very much the day before he died, and when he was dying he made great efforts to articulate something. Only one word was caught, — his last word: it was, JESUS.

He lived and acted under the uniform conviction that religion was the principal thing. He made no forced efforts showing that he wished you to feel that he was thinking of religious things, but you could not be with him long without perceiving that religion was uppermost in his thoughts. The providential goodness of God was an unfailing source of conversation with him. He was deeply impressed with the shortness and uncertainty of life, and with the importance of being ready for death at all times. This led him to incessant efforts for the good of others. Soon after the present Pastor's installation here, Deacon Melledge proposed to go with him to every family in the congregation. In these visits, the Pastor became intimately acquainted with him, and formed an attachment to him which never abated. He had a happy faculty of speaking on religious subjects without formal introductions, conversing as freely on these themes as on others. His disposition was most vivacious and cheerful, his face a benediction, his manifest regard for those whose good he sought always disarming prejudice, winning a way for him to the heart and conscience without conflict. He would make repeated visits to learn if the remarks which he made, the book which he had given, had produced the desired effect. So he "watched for souls." Seldom has one been found in our churches who made it so much his business to seek the salvation of men.*

* One incident will illustrate this. A deputation from several Southwestern Indian Tribes visited Boston in 1837. An immense crowd assembled to witness their exhibition of war-dances on the Common. Our friend obtained a seat on the box of a coach with the driver, to enjoy the sight. Some one who knew him and saw him sitting with the coachman, said to a friend, "I will venture much that he will talk to that man about his soul." When he came down from his seat and found his friends, one of the first things which he said to them was, with his usual earnest manner, "Really, that man has some very serious thoughts; he thinks a good deal about his soul." The excitement in the streets, his curiosity to see all that was passing, and his being an entire stranger to the man, did not prevent him from talking with him about the great salvation. Referring to

It was not to the unconverted only that our friend was faithful. He would mourn over professing Christians who seemed to be negligent, as much as over others: so that his zeal was not a mere endeavor to bring people into the Church. He would speak to men and women about their spiritual condition in a way to bring tears to their eyes, and his words and tones on such occasions are deeply impressed on the memories of some among us. "My dear child," he would say to one who had confessed that he was neglecting secret prayer, "depend upon it this will not do; it will never do; you ought not to live so; there is no oil in your vessel with your lamp; I am afraid you do not love the Bible; if you did, you would not live in this poor state." It was interesting to hear him talk with men who did not observe family prayer. He would reason with them as earnestly as though he were persuading them to do some great thing for their temporal advantage. When a church member was overtaken with a fault, no affectionate, faithful physician or nurse could do more for a patient, than he did to restore such, in the spirit of meekness. He assisted many in their embarrassments, doing it privately and delicately. He advised many as to their children; and his counsels extended sometimes,

the practice of thus speaking a kind word to individuals on the subject of religion, he would say, " In the morning sow thy seed, and in the evening withhold not thy hand; for thou knowest not which shall prosper, whether this or that; or whether both shall be alike good."

in the most suitable and inoffensive way, — coming from an elderly man, — to the subject of personal and domestic habits.*

If there be a name by which one might best express the entire impression which this good man has made upon many hearts, it would be this, — "The Good Church Member." He loved all the Churches of Christ, but he was enthusiastic in promoting the prosperity of the Church where God had assigned him his place of labor. It is true that circumstances in the early history of this Church gave him a peculiar attachment to it, yet his love for it was the offspring of Christian principle and not of accidental circumstances. He had the greatest dislike, and expressed the strongest disapprobation, of roving from one place of worship to another, from love of change, or with no fixed attachments. He used to say to those who thus wandered: " You will never grow ; ' those that be *planted* in the house of the Lord, shall flourish in the courts of our God.' You must take root somewhere if you would grow." †

---

* Turning back at the close of a visit, he kindly said to one whose dwelling was not in all respects so uniformly tidy as he thought a Christian's dwelling should be, " My dear, religion is cleanliness; depend upon it, cleanliness is next to godliness."

† The following will illustrate his habit of doing good to all. Mr. R. W. Staton arrived at our wharves from Torquay, England, in 1835, to find occupation here as a master-workman in freestone. Deacon Melledge, having some business on board the vessel, accosted this stranger, and soon found that he was a professor of religion. He exhorted him to be stead-

The Pastor seldom met Deacon Melledge in the street but he would produce a paper with a list of persons whom he had visited, and would call attention to one and another who he thought were seriously inclined, or were depressed, or were troubled with doubts. He would make an almost incredible number of calls in a short space of time; and this, in part, because he came at once to his object in the call, without formality, and without mingling with it miscellaneous things.

As a member of the Committee for conversing with candidates for admission to the Church, he was discerning and quick in his judgment; charitable, as well as faithful. A favorite question with him to a candidate was: "Do you enjoy such parts of the Word of God as the one hundred and nineteenth Psalm?" adding: "I think a great deal of a spiritual taste." That

fast in the Christian life, and gave him an invitation to worship, the next Sabbath, at our Church. He took the directions for finding the place, but lost them. Walking along to find a place of worship on Sabbath morning, he saw over the door of this house a marble tablet, inscribed, "Erected to the worship of Jehovah, Father, Son, and Holy Ghost." He felt drawn toward the place, and on coming into the porch, he met Deacon Melledge, who, being Treasurer of the Society, was statedly there to receive applications for pews and seats, and to welcome strangers. Mr. Staton soon became a member of this Church, and was a useful teacher in the Sabbath School. He died in 1852, honoring his Christian profession in life and death. Several prominent buildings among us witness to his skill as a worker in stone, viz.: the Boston Athenæum; Bank of Commerce; Shoe and Leather Dealers' Bank; Club House, West Street; Rowe Street Baptist Church; First Presbyterian Church, Harrison Avenue; and the Episcopal Church, Brookline.

Psalm, full of seeming repetitions to a cursory reader, was, to his spiritual mind, sweeter than the honeycomb, because it consists in desires after God.

Few ever enjoyed the Sabbath more than he. It was like a festival; and his feelings toward it are an illustration of what he called a spiritual taste.

He did much to promote the acquaintance of Church Members with each other; saying: " I love to put the coals together, and not let them lie scattered about the hearth."

He was active in bringing individuals, who were not accustomed to hear evangelical instructions, to evening lectures; going home with them after service, as this was the condition upon which their friends allowed them to come. In this way, valuable accessions have been made by him to this Church. It is believed that it was owing to his personal influence, as much as to any means, that a deceased Member of the Church, who, by her benefactions while living, and by her will, has made this Church her almoner,* was originally led to worship here. He himself was a benefactor to the Society, not only in his original contribution toward building the house, but in relinquishing much property in pews to assist the Society in rebuilding it.

All who enjoyed his hospitality united in their admiration of his cheerful, generous disposition, and of the charm which he spread around his fireside. His famil-

---

* Mrs. Ann Lee, (wife of William,) formerly Mrs. John McLean.

iar acquaintance with English hospitality was conspicuous in his treatment of his guests. He sometimes acted almost literally on the injunction of Christ: "When thou makest a feast, call the poor, the maimed, the lame, and the blind." It was affecting to see at his funeral many who were evidently drawn there by the feeling that they had lost one of their greatest benefactors. A colored person, who came and looked at his remains, said: "O! he was a good man! His last charge to me was to be faithful."

He had a forgiving and generous disposition toward those who had injured him. There was a time when he, with others, were subjected publicly to ill treatment, and unworthy imputations were openly cast upon them. While suffering from this source, our friend is known to have contributed privately toward the pecuniary relief of the individual who was the cause of this ill treatment.

He made no pretensions to shining talents; he had none of those eminent qualities which make one distinguished before the great assembly; but we have in him an illustration of the power which there is in goodness of heart, and habits of usefulness, to dispense great happiness, and to make their possessor happy; for he was one of the happiest of men. Though he had good insight into character, he did not indulge in criticisms upon others, being remarkably forbearing and charitable, and even silent, with regard to faults, when duty did not oblige him to speak. He was sagacious in business, industrious, and provident; he passed through life friendly to all men, and conciliating their esteem and love. He was very fond of the young; he would stop them in the street, with kind words of advice and benediction. Many now live who remember him from these accidental greetings.

The days at length came when men are "afraid of that which is high, and fears are in the way;" when "the grasshopper is a burden and desire fails." But the ruling passion of love to others was strong to the end. One of his last calls was upon a member of the Church, to obtain a list of the sick and afflicted. He had a constitutional dread of dying, and seldom ventured to speak of the last mortal conflict. But, as his end drew nigh, he had no terrors; his look and smile made known that he was at peace. It is not a vain repetition to say, that the last word which he uttered was the name "which is above every name."

DEACON GILMAN PRICHARD.

THE Committee would do injustice to their own feelings if no allusion were made to the third Deacon who died in office, — GILMAN PRICHARD.

He was one of that noble band who were sent to us from Park Street Church, — Noyes, Hale, Woodman, and others, — whose influence was so great and salutary in the early history of the Church.

Deacon Prichard had a remarkably well-balanced mind. His conclusions on all important subjects were ever marked with good judgment and prudence. He gave his opinions with modesty, but they were well-considered and firm. His example as a systematic contributor to religious and charitable objects; his consistent, uniform piety, won the affections and secured the confidence of the Church. To all who remember his constant attendance on religious ordinances, his efforts to sustain and aid in the praises of God in the sanctuary, and his labors in the Sabbath School as Teacher and Superintendent, his memory is as ointment poured forth.

MISCELLANEOUS STATEMENTS.

CHANGES IN THE MINISTRY IN BOSTON.

DURING the past twenty-five years, every other Church of our denomination in the city has had one, or two, and, in two cases, three, changes in its ministry. The Baptist Churches have all changed their Pastors within that period. The Episcopal Churches have likewise each had a change of its Rector. In three of the Unitarian Churches, three Pastors remain who have been in office (one originally as colleague) more than twenty-five years.

THE MEETING-HOUSE.

The Meeting-House was remodelled in 1840–41, by raising the roof about eleven feet, reconstructing the tower, renewing the large audience-room, and making the present lecture-room, with the other rooms on that floor. The former lecture-room was several feet below the level of the street. Though by no means inviting, it was the scene of great spiritual blessings.

The successful effort to remodel the house, was made just after one of the most powerful and interesting seasons of religious interest which we have ever enjoyed. We deem it not unsuitable to say, that the effort to rebuild was commenced and carried on chiefly by the present Senior Deacon, whose family had shared richly in this work of grace; his zeal, and that of others, in thus laboring for the House of God, being ascribed by them to their grateful sense of God's goodness.

This House of Worship, and the land on which it stands, were conveyed by deed to a Board of Trustees, for the use of Union Church, by Deacon Nathan Parker, in 1822. The object of the trust deed was to secure the property to the Church, to be occupied by them, secure from perversion, for the worship of the one only living and true God, — Father, Son, and Holy Ghost. It was subsequently found that the operation of the trust deed, excluding Members of the Congregation from participation in the secular affairs connected with religious ordinances, was unfavorable; so that the trust deed was cancelled, and the *Essex Street Congregational Society* was formed, under the Statutes, in 1837, and the property was made over to them.

FREEDOM FROM DEBT.

The Society is free of debt, and its property is unincumbered. By the rebuilding of the house, in 1840, a debt was incurred, which, for several years, was a source of embarrassment. The manner in which this debt was removed is instructive. The American Board of Foreign Missions, at their meeting in Philadelphia in 1841, had recommended to its patrons an increase of twenty-five per cent. in their contributions. When the subject was brought before this Church, doubts were felt whether, in view of our own debt, it was expedient to urge upon the people this recommendation of the Board.

But we quoted, one to another, in behalf of the Board, the words of the prophet to the woman of Zarephath: "Fear not; make me a little cake first, and bring it unto me, and after make for thee and for thy son." We increased our contributions to the Board; this put animation into our hearts for further effort; we prepared a sinking fund for the gradual extinction of the debt, which, in process of time, would have removed it; but, by personal effort on the part of one who joined the Church with the resolution that the debt should be extinguished, it was soon paid, by private subscriptions.

CHARITABLE CONTRIBUTIONS.

In pursuance of a vote of the Church, January twenty-fourth, 1838, records have been kept of all collections in our Society from that year. The result, from 1838 to 1859, inclusive, is as follows:

For Foreign Missions	$65,800.00
Other benevolent objects	59,773.95
	$125,573.95

During the same period, the Meeting-House has been rebuilt, at a cost of about	$20,000 00
Society's Debt extinguished	6,500.00

MEMBERSHIP.

During the last twenty-five years, there have been added to this Church,

On Profession	441
By Letter	379
Previously added	600
Original Members	12
Total in thirty seven years	1,432

There have been

Dismissed during the thirty-seven years	686
Died	213
Excommunicated	33
	932

Whole number of Members from the beginning	1,432
Subtract	932
Present number	500

BAPTISMS.

Three hundred and eighty-one infants and young children have been baptized here since the formation of the Church.

COLLEGE STUDENTS.

The following are the names of those in our Society who have received Collegiate Education:

Joseph S. Ropes,
Henry B. McLellan,
Samuel Salisbury Tappan,
William B. Stevens,
Francis W. Tappan,
Samuel Hosmer,
John P. Gulliver,
Daniel P. Gulliver,
William Sewall,
John A. Vinton,
Frederic Vinton,
Thomas C. Hale,
Robert B. Hall,
Edward L. Rogers,
Albert E. Stetson,
Henry I. Cobb,
James T. Cobb,
Henry Perkins,
Samuel Haskell,
Henry M. Haskell,
William L. Ropes,
Edward G. Miner,
Timothy D. Chamberlin,
Charles F. Thayer,
Francis Parker,
John S. Perkins,

Ormund H. Dutton,
Amory T. Gibbs,
Charles E. Briggs,
Nathaniel H. Broughton,
William L. Gage.
Nathaniel E. Gage,
Edward A. Strong,
Rufus Choate, Junior,
William S. Cogswell,
Evarts Scudder,
David C. Scudder,
Samuel H. Scudder,
Horace E. Scudder,
James A. Littlefield,
William K. Hall,
William H. Dunning,
Arthur Wilkinson, Junior,
William C. Wood,
William H. Adams,
William F. Perkins,
Horace Dutton,
William Henry Lathrop,
Leonard C. Alden,
Alfred O. Treat,
Charles R. Treat.

To these may be added, William H. Beecher and Charles C. Beaman, Students in Theology, they having previously been engaged in business.

This list includes : 1. Those who were born while their parents, one or both, were Members of this Church. 2. Those who were baptized here, the parents being at the time, one or both, Members of the Church. 3. Those who were, with their parents, in the Congregation for a season, one or both of the parents belonging at the time to this Church. 4. Those who were at any time Members of this Church, their parents neither of them being Members.

The list is intended to preserve and cherish a mutual remembrance on the part of the Church, and of those here named, whom it has regarded as in any sense, and for whatever period of time, its children.

It will be interesting to know that, of the fifty-one first named here, thirty-two have been, or were expecting, or at the present time are expecting, to be connected with the sacred office of the Ministry; and, moreover, that with one exception, the parents of all of them were, one or both, in covenant with God as Members of the Christian Church.

DEACONS.

Nathan Parker, elected December eleventh, 1822; died, 1830.

James Melledge, elected December eleventh, 1822; died, 1844.

Josiah Vinton, Junior, elected December twenty-fifth, 1822; dismissed to Braintree, 1829.

John Gulliver, elected September twenty-third, 1825; dismissed to Free Church, 1835.

Charles Scudder, elected February twenty-fifth, 1831.

Gilman Prichard, elected February twenty-fifth, 1831; died, 1833.

George Rogers, elected August seventh, 1835.

Thomas Adams, elected February eighth, 1839; dismissed, with others, at the formation of Mount Vernon Church, 1842.

George W. Thayer, elected April fourteenth, 1843.

George D. Dutton, elected May twelfth, 1848.

SUPERINTENDENTS OF THE SABBATH SCHOOL.

Gilman Prichard,
Charles Scudder,
Jonathan D. Steele,
James M. Gordon,
Henry A. Johnson,
Thomas J. Lee.

INDEX.

	PAGE
PRELIMINARIES	7
PREPARATORY RELIGIOUS EXERCISES	8
EXERCISES AT THE ANNIVERSARY:	
Chant: Selections from the Scriptures	13
Ode, by Mrs. Davies	15
Remarks by the Chairman	21
Address by Mr. Choate	22
Extracts from Mr. Beaman's Poem	39
Hymn, by Miss Spear	41
Remarks by General Oliver	45
Ode, by Mr. Steele	49
Remarks by the Pastor	53
SOCIAL GATHERINGS	56
Address by Deacon George Rogers	57
CONCLUSION	60
CORRESPONDENCE	65
Portrait of Doctor Adams	96
BRIEF HISTORY OF UNION CHURCH	99
Reverend SAMUEL GREEN, (with a Portrait)	102

	PAGE
Deacon NATHAN PARKER	104
Deacon JAMES MELLEDGE	108
Deacon GILMAN PRICHARD	117

MISCELLANEOUS STATEMENTS:

Changes in the Ministry in Boston	118
The Meeting-House	119
Freedom from Debt	120
Charitable Contributions	121
Membership	122
Baptisms	122
College Students	123
Deacons	125
Superintendents of the Sabbath School	125

www.ingramcontent.com/pod-product-compliance
Lightning Source LLC
Chambersburg PA
CBHW020112170426
43199CB00009B/502